Pol[illegible] Theory to Practice

A Complete Guide to Treat Anxiety, Calm Depression, and Regain Social Engagement

Alexis Collins

TABLE OF CONTENTS

FOREWORD

Ever since the polyvagal theory came into the scene slightly over two and a half decades ago, there has been considerable interest in how it can be applied in clinical settings. As part of my scholarly work, I have written quite a lot on the vagus nerve. I have two books out which are essentially self-help guides on how to stimulate the vagal tone and fight off anxiety and inflammation.

For someone to write about the polyvagal theory as authoritatively as Alexis Collins has, they need to have a thorough understanding of the dynamism of the parasympathetic nervous system. The author puts across in such an ingenious way the social engagement system, the third type of nervous system response that operates out of a unique nerve influence.

Alexis has expounded on how Steven Porges' Polyvagal Theory has to a greater extent provided therapists with a platform to assist their clients in reframing their reaction to traumatic events. Reactions have adaptive functions which previously weren't well understood even by compassionate therapists. However, the theory as explained has brought the language through which clients including trauma survivors can express their personal narratives and experiences.

Reading through Alexis' *Polyvagal Theory to Practice*, you get the sense of how complex yet critical the vagus nerve is. Building up as she has from the very foundation of the theory requires mastery and keenness on heart and mind. Alexis has taken the Polyvagal Theory as we know it and linked it with the complexity of emotions, making it easier for anyone to embrace it.

To be honest, if Alexis' book is what I had gotten hold of the first time I learned of the polyvagal theory, I could have understood it in a much clearer way. Where other authors struggle to clear the way, Alexis simply lights the path and brings out the relevance of the theory in helping practitioners and patients understand trauma and related experiences.

As a research scientist, my focus and main interest are on the pathways through which the autonomous nervous system influences the physiological and behavioral processes. This book dedicates a whole chapter to help the audience understand the nervous system and stress responses which I think is incredible. It also discusses at length the social engagement system which is the heartbeat of the Polyvagal Theory.

Alexis' work has shifted my curiosity to the salient features expressed by individuals with psychiatric diagnoses. All through my research work on the vagal complex, I haven't met as many people as Alexis Collins who just comes in and light up the universe of the nervous system. She is a talented researcher and psycho-emotional therapist.

What the author sees in the Polyvagal Theory is essentially a language that parallels her intuitive connectedness with the feelings of trauma patients. The theory has become more of a lens that help practitioners offer the right support to clients and reframe their reactions to their experiences.

As evidenced in Alexis literal works, the Polyvagal Theory has provided a route for transforming narratives of clients from mere documentaries to practical quests for safety. Her current book is an embodiment of the transformative effect of the theory.

I can confidently say that in the *Polyvagal Theory to Practice*, Alexis has recorded tremendous success in transitioning a theory that's neurobiologically based into a practice that everyone who values wellness and internal harmony can't afford to miss out.

Elizabeth Williams
Author of *Daily Vagus Nerve Exercise* and
Activating Vagus Nerve Workbook

INTRODUCTION

The world of medicine is filled with mysteries that provide no easy explanations.

For example, some people are actually allergic to water (Healthline, n.d.), which is rather strange considering the fact that our bodies are around 60% water. However, here is where things enter what I would like to call the "medical twilight zone". These individuals who are allergic to water can actually drink the liquid without any problem. It's the contact they have with water that causes the problem. Even a few minutes in the bath can cause their skin to develop itchy red welts. But why is this condition a mystery? The simple fact is that medical professionals and researchers have no clue what causes it.

Let's take another condition. Imagine a mother holding her newborn baby boy in her arms. It's her firstborn and both parents are filled with joy, pride, and love. The father looks down at his baby boy and can't help but think how his life is complete.

Except that, genetically, his wife is not the mother of the child (Praderio, 2017).

This is not a case of infidelity. Nor is it an example of demonic possession or some sci-fi movie plot that you might think about. No, aliens aren't among us and the Men in Black aren't real. I think.

Back to the story. Imagine the mother looking down at her child and understanding that she is not biologically related to him, even though she gave birth to him. This has actually happened to a few people around the world and the reasons behind the births are still shrouded in mystery.

And then there is the vagus nerve.

Yes, much has been discovered about the vagus nerve over the last few decades. But think about that for just a second. Just the last few decades? That does not seem right, does it? You see, the vagus nerve is part of the nervous system and specifically works alongside the parasympathetic nervous system. The nervous system itself was discovered in the third century by Alcmaeon of Croton, who was a Greek philosopher and medical theorist (Panegyres & Panegyres, 2016). It was he who developed ideas about the human body, most notably the nervous system. His ideas led to lots of discoveries about the nervous system.

However, the stimulation of the vagus nerve and its resulting effects were not studied in detail until 1983 (Roberts & Bullis, 2019)! Imagine that. Researchers had centuries available to them to look into the nerve, yet they could not make detailed observations—or rather, they had not discovered its true potential—until the 20th century. Pretty surprising, isn't it? That is why the vagus nerve remained a mystery for a long time. When researchers uncovered its uses, they were surprised to find a plethora of advantages that the nerve could provide for the body. It was connected to so many areas of the body that not only maintained the body's well-being but the overall health and longevity of the person.

At this point, you might be wondering why I brought up the examples of the mysterious medical discoveries at the beginning of this book. The vagus nerve has been discovered. It isn't a mystery anymore.

Or is it?

The research into the vagus nerve is relatively new. Despite researchers having modern technology to speed things up, they still have quite a bit more ground to cover before they can fully understand all the functions of the nerve. Researchers are still trying to figure out just how many functions the vagus nerve manages. But their abilities are limited as well. To truly understand everything there is to know about the nerve, they have to see it in action. As you might have guessed, that is not exactly a safe method to implement. So, they have to use observations and other ideas to further their research.

But what researchers have already discovered reveals a whole world of wonder and benefits. And those wonders and benefits are what we are going to look into.

There is quite a bit of ground to cover. So, let's get started.

1:

THE AUTONOMIC NERVOUS SYSTEM

The nervous system. If you had to explain what the nervous system is in three words, you could say it is the body's "electrical wiring system".

That seems a bit vague, doesn't it? But it is actually true. And to understand that, you have to think about the wiring system in your house. Each house or apartment comes equipped with a main electrical panel. However, of what use is the panel without the wires? You can switch on the main electrical supply, but without the wires, the signals cannot reach their intended destination. You could flip the kitchen light switch all day, but it is not going to do anything if the right wires don't carry the electrical signal from the switch to the lights.

In your body, your brain is the main electrical panel, sending signals to various parts of the body. The nervous system is the wiring system that connects the brain to the individual parts.

Since the signal starts from the brain, let's focus on that first.

Started From the Brain and Now the Signal's Here

When people try to explain the brain, they often compare it to a computer. That comparison isn't too far from the truth. The brain is responsible for controlling numerous functions, a lot of them simultaneously, including the way you think, feel, talk, and walk. The reason why you know how to swing the racket to hit the tennis ball rather than smack it on your own head is because of the brain. The conversations that you have with your friends and family and the emotions you pour into them are because of the brain. Cooking, cycling, writing, reading, and well, you get the picture.

Our body's functions are reliant on the brain. But that is just one part of the equation. On the other side, you have the nervous system, ensuring that the brain's messages reach its intended destination. The nervous system itself is a complex collection of special cells that are called neurons and various nerves that help carry the signals from the brain.

In order to create such signals, both the brain and the nervous system contain nerve cells called neurons, which are essentially the building blocks of all communication that takes place between the brain and the nervous system. We have about 86 billion neurons to help the brain and the nervous system perform their activities properly.

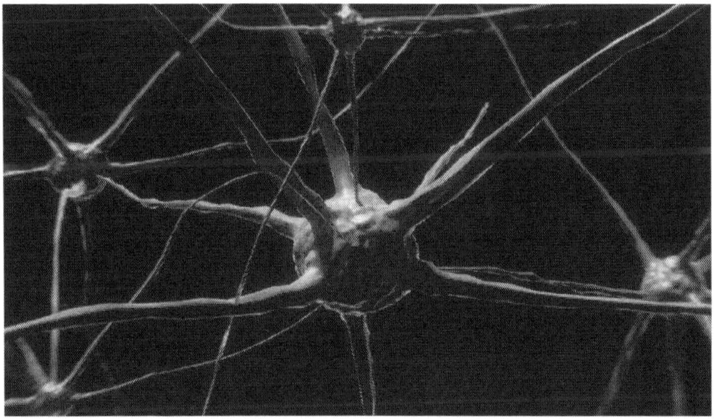

Image 1: The brain creates memories through neurons. Every time a new memory is formed; neurons form new connections in your brain.

Nervous System and Its Two Components

In order for the nervous system to function properly and handle the numerous tasks it is responsible for, it is split into two components:

Central Nervous System: This component of the nervous system includes the brain and the spinal cord.

Peripheral Nervous System: This component comprises the nerves that go through the entire system.

Each of the two nervous systems above are important. But the component more germane to the topic at hand is the peripheral nervous system. Think of the Central Nervous System (CNS) as a superhighway that starts from the top and moves down your body. Now imagine that your organs and other parts of the body are buildings and structures littered on both sides of the highway. However, here is the catch. These structures are not all directly attached to the highway. Some of them are set quite some distance away from the spinal cord. Others, like your fingers, are quite some distance from the center of your body. The only way to connect them to the superhighway is through a network of roads and exits that break away from the superhighway. Those roads and exits form your Peripheral Nervous System (PNS).

Essentially, the PNS contains spinal, cranial, and peripheral nerves; all of which branch out from the CNS. These nerves link the CNS to various parts of the body so that any messages from the brain can flow down your CNS superhighway and reach their intended destination.

At this point, it is important to think of the body as a large organization. One person cannot manage the entire system. You have the founder or CEO of the organization, followed by senior management, followed by the department heads who in turn manage the team leaders. When an organization has a structure, there is a smooth flow of communication from one part to another. This is the same with our body, most notably our nervous system. Because the PNS handles so many tasks, it is further divided into two components.

The Somatic Nervous System

This component of the PNS is responsible for carrying motor and sensory information to and from the CNS. There are two types of neurons in this part of the PNS and they are named after the type of information they carry.

- You have the motor neurons that carry information to and from various muscles in the body. If you notice someone toss a bottle of water at you, the reason you are able to move your hands and position your arms to catch the bottle is that your motor neurons have communicated the message from your brain to your muscles to prevent the bottle from landing on your head. Your motor neurons allow your body to respond to stimuli in the environment by taking physical actions.
- The sensory neurons are responsible for carrying information from the nerves to the CNS. The reason you feel cold during winter or sense the heat as soon as you step into a sauna? Yes indeed. Those are your sensory neurons at work.

The Autonomic Nervous System

Now here is where things might get a little confusing, but do not worry, I'm going to guide you with a diagram at the end of this section. Before we get to that diagram, we need to examine the autonomic nervous system's functions. This part of the PNS is responsible for regulating and managing involuntary bodily functions, such as digestion, heartbeat, blood flow, and breathing. If you perform an action without conscious thought, then you are using the Autonomic Nervous System, or ANS, to make it happen.

Think about those times when you jerk your hand away from an object because it is quite hot or flinch when chilly water touches your skin. All of these actions are involuntary and come under the management of the Autonomic Nervous System.

There are essentially two branches of involuntary movement, highlighted by the two branches of the Autonomic Nervous System:

➢ *The Sympathetic System*

This part of the ANS gets the body ready to expend its energy and deal with any potential or perceived threats in the environment. When you decide to take action, then the Sympathetic System activates a response that increases your heart rate, activates sweat secretion, increases your breathing, dilates the pupils, and increases blood flow to various muscles in the body. All of these changes allow you to react quickly to stimuli in the environment. In certain scenarios, people stay and choose to fight the threat while in other scenarios, people choose to flee and escape from the source of danger. In short, your fight-or-flight response.

➢ *The Parasympathetic System*

Your parasympathetic system helps to manage regular bodily functions, or in other words, those involuntary functions that are activated when your body is at a state of rest. This system also helps you conserve your physical energy and resources. Usually, when a threat has passed, your body does not need to be in a state of high-intensity alertness. For example, let's say you are walking home from work. You spot a shadow in an alleyway heading towards you. Thoughts run through your mind. Is that a robber? Or perhaps a secret assassin here to take you to a hidden laboratory, where you get trained to become a super spy and get to use cool gadgets and save the world? Or maybe…

Oh, wait. It's just a teenager taking a walk. Right. No need to panic or get overly excited.

Now, imagine if your body refused to calm down. Even though you discovered that the threat was not really a threat, your body remains in a state of fight-of-flight. Sounds uncomfortable, doesn't it? It is like having a panic attack that does not end.

Your parasympathetic system slows down your breathing and heart rate, constricts the pupils, and reduces the blood flow to the muscles in order to bring your body back to a relaxed position.

I promised you a diagram to better help you understand the nervous system hierarchy that I presented in this chapter. And so here it is. Do note that this diagram explains the nervous system as mentioned in this book and should not be taken as a medical representation of the system. Medically, the nervous system is far more complex and has numerous branches and connections.

The above diagram gives an overview of the structure that we just talked about.

The Sympathetic and Parasympathetic Systems have numerous other functions that they oversee, each function targeting a specific organ. For some organs, only one of the systems is responsible for a specific function or causes a certain effect. Let us take a look at some of them.

Target Organ/ System	**Parasympathetic**	**Sympathetic**
Digestive system	Increase peristalsis and amount of secretion by digestive glands	Decrease activity of digestive system
Liver	No effect	Causes glucose to be released to blood
Lungs	Constricts bronchioles	Dilates bronchioles
Urinary bladder/ Urethra	Relaxes sphincter	Constricts sphincter

Kidneys	No effects	Decrease urine output
Heart	Decreases rate	Increase rate
Blood vessels	No effect on most blood vessels	Constricts blood vessels in viscera; increase BP
Salivary and Lacrimal glands	Stimulates; increases production of saliva and tears	Inhibits; result in dry mouth and dry eyes
Eye (iris)	Stimulates constrictor muscles; constrict pupils	Stimulate dilator muscle; dilates pupils
Eye (ciliary muscles)	Stimulates to increase bulging of lens for close vision	Inhibits; decrease bulging of lens; prepares for distant vision
Adrenal Medulla	No effect	Stimulate medulla cells to secrete epinephrine and norepinephrine
Sweat gland of the skin	No effect	Stimulate to produce perspiration

Now that we are aware of the nervous system and its various components, let us now narrow our attention to the Parasympathetic System. Because it is in the Parasympathetic System that we shall find an important nerve; the vagus nerve.

2:

THE VAGUS NERVE

To understand the vagus nerve, we need to zoom in and examine the structure that the nerve is part of—the cranial nerves.

I am guessing that you might be confused with the number of times the word "nerve" is mentioned here. Is the cranial nerve part of the vagus nerve? Are they two different nerves that are somehow linked together? How many more nerves are there?

To remove the confusion, we need to first understand that cranial nerves are the nerves that emerge from the brain. The term "cranial nerves" is an umbrella term since it does not refer to a single collection of nerves, but 12 different types of nerves. Though the 12 nerves originate from the brain, they each serve different functions. Let us look at each of the nerves and their functions.

Cranial Nerve	Function
Olfactory Nerve	Smell
Optic Nerve	Sight

Oculomotor Nerve	Controls muscle movements of the eyes
Trochlear Nerve	Controls muscle movements of the eyes
Trigeminal Nerve	Swallowing and chewing food Gives sensations to muscles in the ear
Abducens Nerve	Controls lateral rectus muscle in the eye, allowing us to gaze outwards comfortably
Facial Nerve	Helps control certain facial muscles
Vestibulocochlear Nerve	Assists with balance and hearing
Glossopharyngeal Nerve	Responsible for transmitting information from tonsils, middle ear, throat, and back of the tongue
Vagus Nerve	The nerve responsible for numerous functions that we shall discuss in detail below
Accessory Nerve	Helps with motor functions at the back of the neck
Hypoglossal Nerve	Helps with the movement of the tongue

Among all the nerves mentioned above, our main focus lies on the vagus nerve. This begs the question: Just how important is the nerve? It is not possible for one nerve to have so much influence on the body, is it?

You are going to be surprised.

The term "vagus" is Latin and roughly translates to "wandering," which is an apt name for the nerve. This is because the vagus nerve is the longest nerve among all 12 nerves of the cranial network. It begins its journey at the brain stem and extends all the way to the colon, giving the impression that it "wanders" along the length of the body.

When you look at the nerve broadly, then you become aware of certain functions that are split into two components.

➢ *Somatic Components*

- Helps provide somatic sensory information for certain parts of the throat, the outer section of the ear canal, and the area behind the ear.
- Transmits sensory information to the heart, lungs, trachea, esophagus, larynx, and numerous parts of the digestive tract.
- Plays a minor role in allowing us to sense taste at the back of the tongue (or the root area).

➢ *Visceral Components*

- Helps stimulate the muscles near the larynx, pharynx, and soft palate. Your soft palate is the fleshy region at the roof of the mouth near the throat.
- Plays a key role in stimulating the muscles of the heart. This helps your body to lower the heart rate, bringing it back to a resting state.
- Stimulates involuntary reactions in various regions of the digestive tract, including the stomach, esophagus, and numerous parts of the intestine. These stimulations allow food to pass through your body properly.

When you examine the above functions, then you realize how important the vagus nerve is. You might also wonder why it took such a long time for researchers and scientists to discover the vagus nerve. After all, this nerve is like the VIP of the cranial nerves. There is no way one could have missed its presence.

I agree with your thought process. But there is one thing you've got to understand about the research process. The human body is complex. One has to carefully and patiently observe and study it in order to accurately conclude about its functions. Only when one part of the body has been carefully studied can other related parts also be researched. Additionally, for some body parts, it is essential to have better technology.

Take for example the study of neural activity. One cannot simply look at the brain and see tiny cells moving about. If one could do that, then he or she might as well wear a colorful costume and call him or herself part of the X-Men. Since nobody is in possession of superhuman capabilities, we have to rely on certain machines and gadgets for the purpose. To study the neurons, researchers and medical professionals use a brain-computer interface (BCI), which is also often called a neural-control interface (NCI). In a similar manner, researchers make use of machines called electromyography (EMG) to carefully observe the electrical activity of muscles response to nervous stimulation.

What does that mean?

The Complexity of Discovering Nerves

It's like peering into a body and looking at a bunch of nerves. One can see the various organs, muscles, and areas of the body they are connected to. But what does that tell us other than providing help to those organs, muscles, and areas of the body in some mysterious ways? What do they do exactly? Do they control the parts they are connected to or do they merely provide a certain sensation?

Now you might say, "Dear author. You can't possibly tell me it is that difficult to pinpoint the functions of a few nerves. So, what if there are 12 nerves? Let's say there are 20 nerves, just to round off the number and give some room for any unknown nerves that are yet to be discovered. Still, it shouldn't be that difficult right?"

And there, dear reader is where most people do not see the true extent of the nerve network in our body.

Because the body does not simply contain a dozen or maybe two dozen different nerves; it contains hundreds of them. How many hundreds?

No one knows the exact number.

Fascinating, isn't it? Our own bodies are the hosts of incredible medical mysteries.

Once again, how can this be possible? Perhaps another example might clear the fog of doubt you might have. Imagine you have a giant ball of wires approximately 2 feet in diameter in your hands. In front of you are three panels. You realize that all the wires in your hand are of the same color—red. Now you are told that the bundle you hold in your hands includes a wire for each of the three panels. It is your job to find the right wire for a specific panel. Now you are faced with a dilemma. How are you going to find the right wire? Well, in this case, the solution might be rather simple. You take one wire, attach it to a panel and see if it works. If it does not, then you move on to the next. You keep doing this until you have found the right wire for each panel. Simple, isn't it?

But the same solution cannot be used for nerves. There are numerous nerves and some of them tangled up in such complex ways that it is not easy to simply follow them to their destination and accurately figure out their purpose. At the same time, one cannot exactly attach nerves to various muscles and body parts (like the wire example we just examined above) and see what happens! This is why it becomes rather complex when we try to discover the role of each nerve. Thankfully, researchers are able to map out the major nerves. This is because not only are they available in abundance, but they are easy to spot as well.

Time to apply the above theories about nerves to the vagus nerve.

You are looking at a cluster of nerves. In this cluster, there are 12 unique nerves. When you look at diagrams of nerves, you might see them highlighted in different colors. But that is not how they are in your body.

In fact, let's take a look at your arteries and veins. Everyone knows that arteries are red, and veins are blue. Easy to distinguish between the two, right?

Wrong. Neither veins nor arteries are blue or red. The reason that veins appear blue is that light has to penetrate the skin. And it is this light that is reflected onto our retinas that give the veins their color.

In a similar manner, the vagus nerve does not have a different color when compared to the other nerves in the cranial cluster. When observing them, researchers and scientists have to be extra careful when drawing conclusions about their functions. They have to be certain beyond reasonable doubt that a particular nerve actually does what they think it does.

Now you see why things get complicated when it comes to the vagus nerve.

Back to the Vagus Nerve

The vagus nerve is broadly divided into two branches. You have the dorsal vagus and the ventral vagus.

The dorsal vagus is primitive. This means it has been in existence since the earliest animals roamed the Earth. Which is why, you can find the dorsal vagus in numerous animals, including fish. The dorsal vagus travels down the spine and plays a vital role in controlling our heartbeats and ensuring that they remain within an acceptable range, our lungs, and the stomach in order to aid digestion. It is highly active during a "rest" phase. This does not mean that you have to be asleep. Rather, you could be relaxing on the sofa reading a book or lying on the beach. As long as your body is not involved in too many physical movements, your dorsal vagus becomes active. It also becomes extremely active when your "diving reflex" is activated.

Just what is a diving reflex?

You share this reflex with other members of the mammalian family and the term indicates a set of reflexes that are activated when we hold our breath or when our face is cooled (which happens when we hit the water during a dive). The reflex is a physiological reaction that allows the body to tolerate and manage a lower level of oxygen than it usually consumes.

Three important changes take place during a diving reflex.

Change #1: Heart Rate

The heart rate slows down, a reaction that is called bradycardia, in order to preserve oxygen consumption. Typically, your body's heart rate slows down by 10-30%. However, trained individuals are capable of slowing down their heart rate by up to 50%.

Change #2: Blood Flow

The blood vessels become narrower. Called peripheral vasoconstriction, this narrowing of the blood vessels lowers the flow of blood and it is caused when the blood vessels constrict their walls. But why does the body reduce blood flow? If the body can ensure that limbs and other parts of the body receive reduced blood, then oxygen-dependent organs such as the heart and brain receive enough blood for them to function properly.

Image 2: As soon as you hit the water, your diving reflex gets activated.

Change #3: Pressure

This is one of the most incredible changes that take place. Most people react with surprise when they realize just how much the body is capable of. This third change mostly occurs when you dive deep, but it could also activate if you are swimming in shallow waters. A blood shift takes place, which allows water and blood plasma to pass through circulatory walls and organs. These fluids then settle in the chest cavity in order to protect the vital organs from any rise in pressure as you dive deeper. The lungs begin to slowly fill up with blood plasma, which gets drained out if pressure drops. Why is it essential to maintain pressure? When pressure increases, it becomes increasingly difficult for blood to flow through your lungs. In order to ensure that pressure does not restrict the flow of blood, your body automatically tries to maintain a balance. Of course, remember the blood that is meant to flow here is for your vital organs. Your limbs are still receiving less blood than usual.

It is the training of the diving reflex that has allowed humans to hold their breath underwater for longer. In fact, if we train our bodies properly, then we should be capable of staying underwater without an oxygen tank for as long as six minutes.

But how does the dorsal vagus help the body during a diving reflex? One of the key functions of the dorsal vagus is to assist the body as it swings between relaxation and arousal. The ability to relax becomes supremely important when underwater. The more you panic or feel nervous, the more oxygen pumps through your body and the faster you may need to break the surface to take in air. Being relaxed allows your body to properly distribute the blood to the necessary organs. That way, you are able to swim better and longer.

The body also activates the dorsal vagus when the sympathetic nervous system is aroused too much. Such a heightened state of arousal occurs when the body goes into fight-or-flight mode. In reaction to such a state, the dorsal vagus helps your body return to a state of relaxation. At the same time, it understands that your body's stress levels are so high that bringing it down gradually is not going to make much of a difference. Instead, it pushes the state of your body into relaxation quickly. It's as though your dorsal vagus took a free fall into a relaxed state. Because of the suddenness of the reaction, your body ends up becoming immobile. This is one of the reasons people freeze when they enter into a fight-or-flight mode. They begin to panic too much. Their bodies, which are now trying to control that growing panic and allowing the people to calm down enough to focus on the situation at hand, dive into a relaxation mode. The result is that people seem to "shut down," as though they are in a state of extreme shock.

What About the Ventral Vagus?

This component of the vagus nerve appeared later in the evolution of species and is only present in mammals due to their complex body structures. The ventral vagus has also evolved even further in humans extending into the face to help create facial expressions that are vital in social scenarios and engagement. From joy to fear to disgust to shame, you have a variety of reactions to display on your face.

But the ventral vagus plays a far more important role than just creating facial expressions. The ventral vagus also deals with aspects of pleasure. To be more precise, it helps us react towards pleasurable stimuli. In a way, the ventral vagus helps us become more sociable since we are confident about the way we react to people and situations.

The ventral vagus is the part that actively participates in the social engagement system.

And What Is the Social Engagement System?

The social engagement system is an interaction system that mainly includes the mouth, larynx, ears, and eyes. However, it also incorporates numerous parts of the area above the diaphragm. Essentially, all 12 cranial nerves play some role in the social engagement system, but the four most important participants include the facial, glossopharyngeal, trigeminal, and the vagus.

Smiling, eye contact and the tone of voice have always been considered as crucial for good relationships. It is no wonder that you have numerous personality gurus and social experts stressing on the value of eye contact, the ability to display a wide and honest smile that reaches your eyes, and the tone of voice you adopt when talking to someone. For example, if someone were to talk about a tragedy in their lives, then you wouldn't necessarily adopt a sarcastic tone of voice.

Without the aforementioned motor and sensory reactions and connections, it might just be possible that both explicit and implicit understanding of what is occurring socially will always remain crude. This means that we won't be able to easily discern the meanings and inflections of an individual's message, expression, or reaction. It does not matter how intelligent a person is or how much experience he or she has dealing with social situations; without the right motor and sensory connections, they won't be able to even hold a simple conversation. When the social engagement system fails, things might be grossly misunderstood, or expressions might be greatly enhanced. For example, if an individual shows even a modicum of hostile behavior, we might think that he or she possesses violent tendencies. This is because the person does not have the necessary social engagement system to moderate his or her reactions.

Let's take an example of this. Imagine that you are talking to a person about a sensitive topic. As you continue your discussion, you express an opinion that the listener might disagree with. In normal social scenarios, when the listener might have full control of our social engagement system faculties, he or she might control the feelings of displeasure that might arise in him or her. However, without a proper social engagement system, the person might not be able to control his or her reactions, because the system does not know how to.

Image 3: Being aware of your emotions allows you to properly engage people in a conversation.

But what does it mean for a system to "know" how to function properly?

To answer the above question, let us go through the steps that lead to an expression or reaction using a simple example.

You are having a conversation with your friend. Halfway through, your friend says something that is perceived as a positive remark. Your brain recognizes the remark and decides that you should show happiness in response to that remark. This message is sent to the social engagement system and it, in turn, regulates the necessary muscles to make you smile.

Simple, isn't it?

Now, what happens when the social engagement system does not work properly? When your brain tells the nerves to react positively, they simply try to create a positive reaction. Because the system does not know how to form a smile, you end up creating something that looks like a cross between a frown and a grin. I'm guessing that is definitely not your idea of a positive reaction.

Some of the motor and sensory components of the fact are voluntary and are therefore in our control, and some are not. We can show concern and perhaps even disgust, but the expression of true shock and surprise is involuntary. Some expressions are both voluntary and involuntary. For example, we can control a smile, but giving a genuine smile is something that we do involuntarily. Of course, we can train ourselves to give a warm smile, but we are not actually controlling the involuntary aspects of the expression. Rather, we are mimicking the involuntary smile response while hoping that the smile we can voluntarily give is as honest as possible.

Because the vagus nerve is one of the most important players in the social engagement system, it utilizes the ventral vagus to perform the necessary tasks. But since we are on the topic of reactions, it might also help if we dived deeper into understanding emotions as well, since they play a vital role.

3:

THE POLYVAGAL THEORY AND EMOTIONS

When Dr. Stephen Porges was looking into the vagus nerve and its functions, he would never have imagined that he would be responsible for developing a theory that would change the way we examine our body's nervous system.

The Polyvagal Theory splits the autonomic nervous system into three branches. These branches have evolved considerably from primitive animals and are now in their most developed stage in us humans. When we understand these branches, we are able to get a deeper insight into the way in which we are able to assess stressful situations and react to them accordingly.

The Complexity of Emotions

We often like to consider our emotions as something ethereal, mysterious, and complex. We cannot easily identify the way they work.

But in reality, our emotions are fairly simple mechanisms. They are our reactions to certain stimuli, whether those stimuli are external or internal. An example of an external stimulus is when someone says something to you, and you display an emotion in response. On the other hand, an example of an internal stimulus is where you realize that you have an upset stomach and you begin to display emotions in response to that.

Normally, our nervous system is always functioning in the background. It is subtly controlling our bodily functions and regulating our stress responses so that we can focus on other things, such as ordering our favorite drink at the cafe, enjoying a nice TV show, or having a wonderful conversation with someone. In other words, the nervous system is constantly influencing our emotions.

When it comes to our emotional response towards stressful situations, the Polyvagal Theory concludes that our primal need to stay alive is more important to our body than any other form of thought. That is why we often lose track of rational behavior and our ability to maintain our emotions when are faced with stressful situations. Our nervous system takes over rational thought and begins to go through a series of steps. Each step represents one of the three branches of the autonomic nervous system.

We are going to look deeper into these three branches in the next chapter. This is because it might get a little confusing if we suddenly dive into the complexities of the three branches. Let's begin by getting to know more about how our nervous system reacts to stressful scenarios.

The Lion and the Deer

One of the best ways to understand how we handle stress is to examine animals. This is because animals display the simplest form of fight-or-flight responses that we exhibit.

If you have ever watched an Animal Planet documentary on lions and the way they stalk their prey, then you might be aware of what usually happens. The documentary often starts with a group of deer grazing or drinking water by a small pond. Suddenly, one of them looks up, as though it sensed something that the others didn't. The deer's sympathetic nervous system has been activated, sending the necessary chemicals throughout its body to focus its senses. Now the entire group is hyper-alert. Their ears twitch, trying to catch any sounds that are out of the ordinary. Their heads are moving constantly, as though they want to make sure that they get visual confirmation of the threat in the environment.

After a while, the lion springs into action. It begins the chase as it runs towards the group. It has so many targets to choose from, so right now its main priority is to get to the group as soon as possible. One particular deer is singled out. When the deer realizes that it is the target of the hunt, it begins to run. Earlier, its sympathetic nervous system was on alert mode. Now it realizes that the threat is real and that it is in danger.

Eventually, the deer is caught. The lion begins to drag it towards its cubs. At this point, the deer's parasympathetic system kicks in and the deer goes limp. It realizes that it has been caught and there is no point in worrying about the situation. Rather, it chooses to play dead to throw the lion's attention off course.

When the lion brings the deer back to its cubs, they play with the animal before eating it. If the lion becomes distracted, then the sympathetic system of the deer starts up again. The deer lifts itself up, as though it has returned from the dead and sprints away to safety.

Immobilization

When humans used to live in caves, they were always on the lookout for predators. Their lives depended on the fact that they were alert. If they lost their focus for even a few brief moments, they could be on the menu of a hungry predator. But their sense of alertness was not just reserved for beasts. They used their heightened awareness to keep track of their environment so that they didn't accidentally step on venomous plants or fail to recognize changes in weather to flee from an incoming storm. When their senses were on high alert, they would freeze in order to better assess the threat. They would try and pick out noises, check for scents, and look out for anything out of the ordinary in the environment.

This is what happens during the first stage of a stress response.

The immobilization is the most basic step. The vagus nerve realizes that there is a threat in the environment and your dorsal vagus takes over, immobilizing you completely in order to help you gauge the threat. It feels as though your sympathetic nervous system is not allowed to increase the fight-or-flight response threat levels just yet. Not until you are able to properly understand what is going on.

There is another purpose for the dorsal vagus to immobilize you. To understand this purpose, it is first important to look into a part of the brain that helps greatly in our fight-or-flight response: The hypothalamus.

The Hypothalamus

The hypothalamus is a fairly small region in the brain that is located at its base. Despite its size, however, the hypothalamus plays an important role in numerous functions such as:

- Releasing hormones
- Maintaining daily physiological cycles
- Regulating emotional responses
- Controlling appetite
- Managing sexual behavior
- Regulating body temperature.

It is the hypothalamus that sends a signal to the sympathetic nervous system that there is a threat in the environment. The hypothalamus then releases numerous hormones, the most important of which is the hormone cortisol. When your body releases cortisol, it increases the heart rate in order to supply your body with the required amount of blood to help you feel the situation, should you choose to do so. At the same time, the hypothalamus tenses your body, getting it ready to spring into action. It helps more blood to pass into the brain, making the organ hyper-alert in order to process information in the environment. In short, your body is in a high state of stress.

How Is the Dorsal Vagus Involved in This Process?

When your body becomes alert, your dorsal vagus intentionally immobilizes you so that you are better able to process the information you receive from the environment. If you are in a state of motion, you are distracted by too many actions. You have to balance your body, make sure you don't bump into objects, maintain your speed, and perform numerous calculations in order to move properly. When your brain handles these calculations, it is too overwhelmed to notice what is happening around you. However, if you were standing still, then your brain is only focused on one task; finding out the source of the threat.

However, there is another reason why you freeze. When you are immobile, you are conserving as much energy as possible. If you simply start moving, then you conserve energy, making you tired for no reason. In order to make sure you have sufficient energy to use if you decide to start running, the dorsal vagus helps you recognize the threat. If there is no threat, then it was just a false alarm and your body begins to relax. Your energy is conserved. However, if there is a threat, then energy is diverted to the most essential parts of your body to aid your flight.

Mobilization

And now, we enter the next phase of the fight-or-flight reaction. Remember that if you perceived that there was no threat in the environment, then you won't reach this stage. You simply return to a relaxed state and go back to doing what you were originally engaged in.

However, when your brain realizes that there is indeed a threat in the environment, then your body is ready to react. You either decide to take a stand against the threat or you decide to flee from the threat.

Each reaction is based on millions of calculations performed by your brain at the same time.

But what if things are not so simple? Could there be a situation where we are unable to process information properly? As a matter of fact, there is.

There Is Nothing Normal About Normalcy Bias

Imagine this scenario. You are on a Boeing 747 airplane as it is just about to approach the runway for landing. The landing gear has been deployed and you hear and feel the deep rumble as the tires make contact with the ground. The 747 taxies along the runway before slowing down. Now begins the tedious process of slowly taxiing towards the designated arrival gates for the plane. You cannot wait for the plane to stop. You see hundreds of passengers around you taking out their cellphones, talking to their family members, checking their belongings, and simply performing actions to prepare themselves for the exit procedures.

Without warning, a shockwave ripples through the airplane. Heat and pressure tear into your flesh. You hear a loud noise that almost sounds like two trains have collided with each other. The noise is deafening, causing your eardrums to take in severe damage. An explosion follows this noise, steams of flames trying to get into every space and crevice in the plane. You see fire above your head and beneath your feet.

Now, try to ask yourself this question: If you find yourself in such a scenario, what would you do? You might be thinking that you would immediately start taking action, trying to look for water or maybe try and save people. Or perhaps you might think that your first reaction would be to panic and try and escape the inferno. Or you could even start screaming on top of your voice in sheer panic.

However, there is another possibility, one that is strange and at odds with rational behavior.

The above scenario did actually happen. In 1977, two airplanes crashed into each other while one was still taxiing along the runway. A KLM flight asked to be cleared for takeoff. At the time, visibility was extremely low due to thick fog covering the airport. The control tower made a quick decision; they gave a go-ahead signal for the KLM flight, not realizing that a Pan Am aircraft was still taxiing along the same runway. The result was that the KLM crashed into the Pan Am flight at 160 miles an hour as it was taking off. This caused the KLM flight to bounce off the Pan Am aircraft, lose control, and then eventually crash in a fiery explosion. Rescue teams could see the glow of flames through the fog and headed in the direction, completely ignoring the Pan Am aircraft, which at that moment was slowly becoming engulfed in flames.

When paramedics and rescue teams eventually reached them, they were able to rescue a few passengers but mentioned something odd when describing the scene much later. According to them, the passengers had a full two minutes to remove their seatbelts and jump out of the huge hole that had appeared on one side of the aircraft. During that time, several dozen people simply failed to take action. They were unable to break free of their paralysis. Here is the kicker: These people were not in a state of shock.

Psychologists studying this behavior discovered something completely strange about people who experience disasters. When they are witnessing the situation unfold, their brains become so overwhelmed with ambiguous information that they just don't do anything at all. They simply become immobile and refuse to do anything. Their brain just seems to shut down.

In many cases, you become unable to deal with the copious amount of stress and anxiety. Your brain cannot simply handle the information that it is receiving. In such cases, your brain knows that you are not in any danger when things are safe and expected. Your brain then engages in a self-soothing behavior, convincing itself that everything is fine. It begins to engage in normal habits because the more it believes that things are normal, the more it can manage your stress and anxiety levels. This is what normalcy bias is. It is a state of mind where your brain is attempting to make you believe that everything is okay.

During a fight-or-flight response, you evaluate the situation and when you perceive a threat, you immediately begin to take action. You only return back to a state of normalcy when the threat has passed or you have dealt with it.

Remember how we explained that the dorsal vagus relaxes you to a point where you become immobile?

When your brain has entered into a state of normalcy bias, then there is a jumble of information. Your dorsal vagus tries to calm the rising stress and anxiety in your body. But when you enter the immobilization stage, the information that you receive is too much for your brain to handle. It cannot sift through the information to decide what is valuable and what should be discarded for the moment.

Instead of choosing to go through all the information at its disposal, it decides to bring you to a normal state. Your brain does this because it believes that if you reach a state of normalcy, then it can go through the information in a reasonable, calmer state. Your anxieties won't get in the way of the brain's evaluation and investigative process.

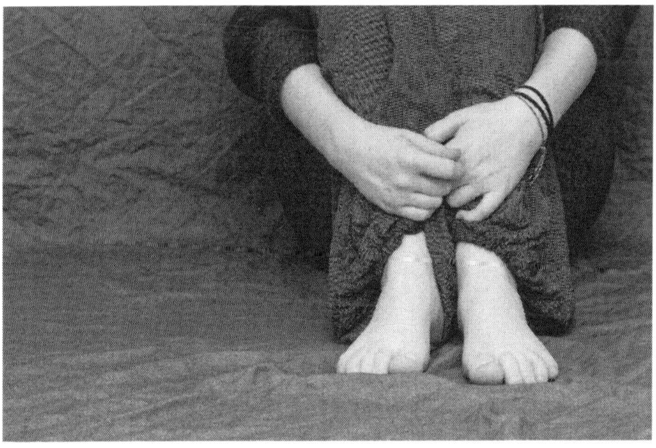

Image 4: In some cases, people who are affected by normalcy bias sit down and make themselves comfortable. They simply want to make themselves feel normal.

Training Fight-or-Flight

Now, you might wonder how it is that police officers and firemen don't enter normalcy bias. After all, don't they go through stressful situations on a daily basis?

Here is something you should know about your brain; it does not do anything it is not aware of. In other words, the way it forms ideas and conclusions are based on information that it already has. Police officers and firefighters are trained every day to handle stressful situations. Firemen use daily practice drills to train themselves into getting into action as quickly as possible after they hear the emergency alarm go off. They do this so many times that their brains form a habit to get them into action even before they have fully processed the crisis they are about to deal with. This allows their brain to forget thinking about getting prepared since that is performed automatically by the firemen. The brain's computing power is then reserved for other information, thus preventing it from becoming overwhelmed.

Have you ever been in a situation where you are walking outside, and someone falls to the ground? One or two people might rush to the person to help while others may continue walking as though nothing has happened? This too is a result of the normalcy bias. The fight-or-flight instincts kick in because people are wondering why someone would fall down. Is there a larger threat that they should be aware of? The dorsal vagus sends them into a sudden state of relaxation. However, at this point, other social cues take over.

Why did the person fall? Is the person hurt? Should someone help the person get up? Should I help the person get up? But wouldn't that be embarrassing? What if I try to help the person and slip myself? What if I am about to reach the person but someone else comes there faster, making me feel so stupid in the middle of the street? Perhaps I could stop and take a look?

As you can see, the brain is already overloaded with information and simply forces a normalcy bias onto you. You could say that it is your brain's way of saying, "Could you please shut up? I'm trying to focus here!"

If you would like to override such behaviors, then you need to first examine yourself. Try to train yourself or your thoughts to react to situations in a particular way. Let's take the above example. You can train yourself to reach out to someone when they fall down. However, you cannot train yourself daily as firemen do. After all, it's not every day you come across a person falling down randomly on the street. In such situations, you can train your mind instead. Try to think about all the reasons that prevent you from helping someone in need. Then slowly answer them while instilling the idea in your mind that helping others is okay, even if it leads to an embarrassing situation.

Does Normalcy Bias Kick in All the Time?

No, it doesn't. When you see a lion chasing you, your brain quickly jumps to a conclusion. You know lions are dangerous. You know that if they catch you, then you are probably going to be served extra rare to the lions and their families. All of this information goes through your brain quickly. It is as if your brain is keeping a checklist and ticking off boxes one by one.

Lion dangerous? Check. Lion bad? Check. Escape from lion good? Check.

All of the above checks are performed so quickly, that in most cases, you have no idea that your brain actually performed them. The result is that you are left with the conclusion: Run.

In order to support the conclusion, the brain prepares the required emotions and chemical reactions in your body. Imagine if you saw a lion chasing you and you suddenly found it so funny that you wanted to laugh out loud. That would be wrong timing on your brain's part, which is why it creates a feeling of fear instead. This fear is then translated into action as you want to get as far away as possible from the source of that fear. This is why you typically enter the mobilization stage of the fight-or-flight process. When your brain understands the danger you are in, it immediately reacts.

Fear or Normalcy Bias

Does that mean that every time you freeze, it is a case of normalcy bias? That's not true at all. Sometimes, even fear can paralyze a person.

Have you heard of the idea that people become too scared to move? That can actually happen. Sometimes, fear becomes such a strong response that the brain is unable to focus on anything else other than the fear itself. This causes the entire body to become paralyzed by inaction.

Guess what you have to do in order to free yourself from this fear-induced paralysis? According to psychologists, taking a few deep breaths stimulates the vagus nerve, which in turn stimulates the parasympathetic nervous system to "unclamp" the grip of fear (Bergland, 2014). We are able to move more freely and think more clearly.

Social Commitment

This is the final stage of the fight-or-flight response. This stage could also come before the immobilization stage. However, since it is a return to a normal stage, it occurs when your fight-or-flight response realizes that there is no threat in the environment to worry about. This stage is activated by the ventral vagus when the brain realizes that you are safe and sound.

In the evolution of human beings, the third step of the stress response occurred much later when language and complex forms of communication were introduced. No longer did humans have to merely grunt and huff in order to communicate. We became more sociable as we discovered newer tools, technologies, and ideas. We developed societies and laws. We began to explain the skies, stars, and the things that we found around us.

Granted, we started with mythical symbolism and vague explanations for some of the phenomenon we saw around us. For example, thunder was equated to a sign of the wrath of the gods. Over time, as we became more intelligent, we were able to explain what we experienced much better. This led us to create more words to express ourselves. Fast forward to the present day where technology surrounds us, and we have more ways to communicate than ever before. Language has evolved to a stage where we can express and explain ourselves in countless ways. This allowed us to better evolve as social creatures.

Because of our social evolution, our ventral vagus began to play an important role in our fight-or-flight response. When we feel a certain threat, we often depend on social cues to explain the situation. If we see people running in fear all around us, then we know that things are truly bad. However, if we look around and notice that people are relatively calm, then we realize that the threat we feel is not something we should be concerned about.

When we feel safe, we begin to connect. We use our social and communication experience to walk around casually, smile at people, make small talk, and do everything that we would do in a non-threatening situation.

Image 5: We are most sociable when we feel that the environment that we are part of is safe.

But isn't there more to these steps than is actually mentioned here? As a matter of fact, there is. And we are going to take a look at that in the next chapter.

4:

THE NERVOUS SYSTEM AND STRESS RESPONSES

In the previous chapter, we looked at three stages of your stress response. We glossed over the stages and covered the essential points briefly. However, in this chapter, we are going to delve into their characteristics, features, and functions.

The Red Zone: Immobilization

We had looked at how your fight-or-flight instincts kick in automatically when your brain perceives a threat in the environment.

I had earlier shown you a simple example of how fight-or-flight responses become activated in an animal. Let's examine in detail the process that takes place during such a response.

The Will to Fight-or-Flight

We are all aware of the first step in this process. Your sympathetic nervous system is activated, and a rush of hormones flood your body. But what happens next?

Your sympathetic nervous system first stimulates your adrenal glands. These glands play a vital role in producing hormones that are essential for our very survival. They also produce sex hormones and cortisol. And two of the most well-known hormones that they also release are adrenaline and noradrenaline. These two hormones increase your rate of breathing, heart rate, and blood pressure. At this time, certain physiological changes begin to occur in your body.

➢ Breathing and Heart Rate

Because of the increase in your breathing and heart rate, energy is being pumped throughout your body. This is your body getting ready to take action.

➢ Flushed or Pale Skin

This situation is similar to the "diving reflex" that we had talked about. Your body reduces the flow of blood to the surface areas of your body and to your extremities. This is done in order to make sure that your arms, legs, brain, and muscles, which are the parts of your body that you are going to be using the most to deal with the threat. At the same time, your body's ability to clot blood also improves in order to ensure that you do not lose too much blood when you sustain an injury. For this reason, it might seem that the individual has taken on a pale or sometimes sickly complexion when they first enter into fight-or-flight mode. However, the person might alternate between a pale and flushed complexion as the blood rushes to his or her brain and head.

➢ *Dilated Pupils*

Your brain wants to make sure that it gets to grab as many visual cues from the environment as possible. In order to do this, it dilates your pupils. When your pupils dilate, you take in more light from the environment. The images become sharper and you are able to distinguish between various objects much better.

➢ *Trembling*

Your muscles become primed for action. They become tense. This tightness of the body can cause shaking or trembling in the body. You also begin to tremble and shake once the adrenaline leaves your system after the threat has passed or your brain relaxes.

The Accuracy of Fight-or-Flight

Fight-or-flight response happens automatically. However, that does not mean that it can accurately predict the situation. What does this mean?

Sometimes, your brain activates the fight-or-flight response even when there is no real threat in the environment. This happens when an individual suffers from a certain emotional or psychological condition. Phobias are an example of one such psychological condition.

For example, if a person was afraid of the dark, then his or her fight-or-flight response would kick in as a result of that fear. When they step out into the dark to reach their bedroom, their instincts make them see things in the dark that aren't there, misunderstand certain objects or lights as something else, or simply jump at almost any noise they hear. The fight-or-flight response has already been activated. The body is already feeling the stress of the response. In some cases, if this heightened state of response does not settle down quickly enough, it could lead to a serious case of a panic attack.

The Characteristics of the Red Zone

➢ Feigning Death

Our ancestors would often use various types of weapons, tools, and projectiles in order to deal with predators or threats. However, when they knew that none of the tools that they possessed would help them in certain aspects, they would begin to rely on other tactics. For example, they would lie still until the threat had passed. You might notice this behavior in other animals as well. We had taken the example of the deer earlier that simply pretends to lie still and "play dead" in order to throw off the lion.

This works with many animals. You might have read or heard of the fact that if you lie still during a bear attack, then the bear will lose interest in you and walk away. This is true, for the most part. You can only play dead in front of a mother bear trying to protect its cubs. When it sees that you are no longer a threat, it will leave you alone. However, if you are being chased by a ferocious or hungry bear, then lying dead is like offering yourself as a sacrifice. Regardless, the idea of lying still actually does work in certain scenarios and is used by many animals such as the Virginia opossum (which is where the phrase "playing possum" comes from).

As human beings exited their living accommodations in caves and transferred to glass, brick, and mortar houses, things changed. No more were we hunted by wild beasts. We didn't need to lie still and play dead. Yet the instinct still remained. Hundreds of thousands of years of honing our fight-or-flight instincts have caused certain reactions, such as immobility, to remain. We just don't always use it against physical threats; we also use it against mental ones.

People who suffer from PTSD and trauma often experience a fight-or-flight response when no such response is required. Certain sights, smells, and even sounds remind them of a past incident that caused them anxiety, placed them in a dangerous situation, or caused them fear. Sufferers can experience these stimuli in various ways. They could be simply standing in a crowded subway station and all of a sudden, they are wracked by a sudden uneasiness that keeps escalating in intensity. Eventually, they are hyperventilating and suffering from a panic attack.

We already understand that fear can paralyze people into inaction. Physical sensations start to occur. We experience strange feelings in the pit of our stomach and our throat might go dry. Sometimes, we end up breathing shallowly. But one of the most important characteristics of fear is that it overrides all rational thought. At this point, the brain is unable to form a solution. It resorts to a reaction that is old and was regularly used by our ancestors: Playing dead. In this case, we just freeze.

But can't our bodies simply choose to run? Shouldn't that be a form of reflex action? Our bodies are not good at telling the difference between real and imagined threats since the brain is in control of trying to sort out fact from fantasy. Since the brain is completely occupied, our bodies simply don't do anything. They freeze.

We are going to look deeper into trauma and PTSD in a later chapter. For now, a brief understanding of how they work helps us understand what makes us freeze.

➢ *Releasing Hormones*

Cortisol, adrenaline, norepinephrine, and epinephrine are some of the hormones that are released in order to help us fight or flee from the threat.

One common misconception that people have about adrenaline is that it reduces the intensity of pain that one feels, but that is not true. In fact, in a study conducted at the Department of Medical Psychology at the Maastricht University, researchers discovered that adrenaline can actually increase the level of subjective pain that a person feels (Janssen, Arntz, & Bouts, 1998). The researchers used various factors, such as threshold to heat pain, the result of electrical stimulation on heart rate, the response of the individuals to pressure pain, and skin sensitivity to explore people's response to subjective pain.

You might be thinking, "Wait just a minute, author. I have experienced this myself. I got injured and I felt the pain way later, once the situation had been dealt with." I agree with you. But the key part in the above statement is "once the situation had been dealt with."

You see, adrenaline does nothing to curb the sensation of pain. It elevates the mind's concentration away from the pain. This means that during a stressful situation, you focus more on other things than the pain. Your attention becomes completely engaged with the source of the threat, finding a solution, or even facing the threat head-on that sensations of pain are placed in the backseat while the threat that you are facing becomes your primary focus. Once the threat has passed, your body relaxes, and your brain focuses inwards. It does this because it needs to ensure that your muscles and organs return back to normal. As it places attention inwards, its focus returns to the area of injury. And that's when you begin to feel the pain.

Our bodies are pretty remarkable, aren't they?

➢ *Emotions*

On an emotional level, there is a sense of dissociation. We feel disconnected from the world. If we are not able to discern the source of the threat, then we experience a sense of hopelessness.

Some people experience shame. When they enter fight-or-flight, the spotlight turns on them. They become self-aware. If they don't know what caused the threat, then they begin to blame themselves. They think that they are stupid for even falling into such a mess as the one that they find themselves in.

Shame is often a result of self-blame. This is also the reason why people act differently in social situations. For example, if people are using a public restroom and someone else enters, they are more likely to wash their hands properly, especially if they were about to simply rinse their hands and walk away. They do this because they are self-aware of their actions. When an observer enters the restroom, the people who were about to simply rinse their hands feel like they were caught doing something wrong. They begin to blame themselves for even thinking of leaving the restroom without washing their hands properly. Their self-blame results in feelings of shame.

Others might even look like they are spacing out. This is another result of their brains overwhelmed with fear or information. In the case of fear, people might look like they are transfixed. If there is an overwhelming amount of information, then normalcy bias kicks in and people look "spaced out."

Some people might experience a sense of claustrophobia or a feeling that they are "trapped." When their brain begins to look for solutions and it does not find any, the situation feels beyond their control. They feel like there is nothing they can do, and because of that, some people experience a sensation of "walls closing in to trap them."

➢ *Bowel Movements*

We might feel nauseous, throw up entirely, urinate, or even defecate. It is as though our bowels and our digestive simply decided to take a vacation because of the fight-or-flight situation. But the reality is that there is a biological reason for the loss of our bowel functions.

Digestive processes and bowel movements require energy. In a fight-or-flight situation, every bit of energy is valuable. The body does not want to waste any energy on things that it does not consider important for survival, which is why keeping your pants clean is the least of its worries.

➢ *Tightness*

At this point, we know that when the body goes through stress, it tenses up in anticipation of the threat. This tensing of the muscles is essentially what causes you to become immobilized. However, it is not merely the muscles that tense up.

In your throat are ringed-shaped muscles on either end of the esophagus. The esophagus begins at your throat and then ends up at the stomach. One of the ringed-shaped muscles can be found at the point where your throat and esophagus meet and is called the upper esophageal sphincter. Another ringed-shaped muscle can be found at the point where your esophagus merges into the stomach and is called the lower esophageal sphincter.

The main purpose of these two ringed-muscles is to open to allow the food to pass through and close when the food has entered the esophagus or stomach. This prevents the food from going back into your mouth. They also open up during a gag reflex, nausea, or when you feel like vomiting to allow food to exit your system. These ringed-shaped muscles are also two of the muscles that become tense during a fight-or-flight response. This is why you might feel tightness in your throat and an inability to swallow properly. This tightness also affects your vocal cords since the muscles in the surrounding area are not moving properly. Due to the lack of movement, you are unable to form words properly. It is for this reason that people find themselves unable to speak properly during a fight-or-flight response.

The Alert Zone: Mobilization

One of the things to understand about this part is that just because we are able to move does not mean that we move in a manner that might be appropriate for the situation.

Some people actually end up curling up in a ball and lying down on the floor. For example, a person might see a gang of thugs out to get him. Rather than bolt, the person might sit down, place his hands over his head to protect his soft spots, and hope for the best. A lot of these reactions are unconscious. The brain reacts in a way that it thinks is ideal for the situation. This is also the reason why people end up in normalcy bias, even when they are in the mobilization stage.

This begs the question: Just how powerful is our subconscious mind? After all, the brain performs millions of calculations subconsciously in order to decide whether a threat is real or not. But aren't we in control of our thoughts in the end?

Subconscious Versus Conscious

What most people don't realize about the subconscious mind is that it works in a clandestine manner. We often think that everything we do is a result of rational thought and behavior. However, that is far from the truth.

Let me give you an example. You are returning home after visiting your favorite store. On your way, you realize that you forgot to get mayonnaise, which was the very reason you had headed out to the store in the first place. Ah well, too bad. You might get it on your next trip. For now, you are just going to settle with a mayonnaise-free sandwich. Thoughts about sandwiches make you think about that incredible cafe you had visited with your friends. Speaking of friends, wonder what they are up to this evening? Perhaps you should give them a call. Maybe it would be best if...

Huh? Hold on just a minute. You have already reached home. That is strange. You barely recollect the journey. It's as though your body was moving automatically.

What you have just experienced was a psychological phenomenon called highway hypnosis. In such a case, your subconscious mind takes over your bodily functions, including movement, while your conscious mind is left to tackle all the insipid thoughts running through your mind.

I could give you another example that you are doing right now as you read this book.

Think about it. You are reading the words on this page. But what about your posture? How is it that you are reading without your lower lips drooping and you slobbering all over your top? All of these little actions are controlled by your subconscious mind as you keep your conscious mind focused on the task at hand.

We often believe that the conscious mind is supreme. We are confident of the fact that it can override the impulses of the subconscious mind. But in reality, our subconscious mind has a lot more influence on our decisions.

How is this important for fight-or-flight? Quite important.

You see, our subconscious minds use the power of priming to come to a conclusion. When a stimulus in the past affects your behavior in the present, then it is called priming. This happens to you every day, even when you don't realize it.

Think about this example. You are walking down the street, paying attention to the emails on your phone. It is going to be another long day and you are frankly not looking forward to it. You turn a corner and you immediately spot a homeless man. You pause, realize that he could do with a warm meal today, and hand him enough money to buy a nice meal and perhaps even a warm cup of coffee.

But why did you do that? Was it because it was the right thing to do? Was it because you at some point in your life, you were living on scraps and you could empathize with the homeless person's situation? Or was it because you realize that humanity could do well by being more kind to each other?

Sure, if I ask you to come up with a reason, you probably might. However, your response to the homeless person's situation happens within a few seconds.

If you decided to think about the situation rationally, then perhaps your thought process would be something like this.

There is a homeless man on the street. It looks like he is asking for a little money.

↓

I can see by looking into the container he is using to collect cash that he hasn't been shown too much kindness today.

↓

Should I help him today? In that case, how much should I give him? Would $20 be enough? Should I make it $50? Perhaps $100 is a good amount. If I give him $20, then he might drop by the supermarket nearby and buy a few items. With that much money, I think the most he might be able to get is a loaf of bread, instant noodles, a cup of coffee, and maybe a small sandwich. Should I tell him what to buy with the money?

↓

No, I think that would be too awkward and strange. After all, I cannot dictate his life. I shall give him $50, just so he can buy food later if he has any money left.

↓

I will take out my wallet and take out the cash. I shall hand it over to him. Is it the right thing to do by handing the money to him? Or should I put it in the container and accept his thanks?

But that is not what happens, is it? You look at the homeless person and you are thinking about your next course of action. Suddenly, there is a thought or image in your mind that makes you realize that you should do the right thing. Perhaps the thought was of your childhood or a previous financial situation. Perhaps it was about something you read online about helping people or a movie you watched recently that changed your perspective of the world. It could even be an emotion; the warm feeling of compassion. It could be anything. But it instantly flashes in your mind.

Where did that thought, memory, or emotion come from? Did you consciously sift through all your memories and choose the one that was appropriate for the situation? No, you didn't. It was as though your mind was ready with the right thought or emotion.

Now I would like you to think back on all the times you involuntarily formed a response. It could have been the time when another vehicle cut you off as you were driving to work, and you responded in frustration or anger. It could have been a time when someone asked you something and you shrugged in response to indicate that you were not interested in conversing with them. During all those moments, your conscious mind was engaged with another task. When something else happened at the same time, you unconsciously reacted, eager to get back to your original point of focus.

What has happened is that your unconscious mind primed you with suggestions on how to react using memories, thoughts, and emotions. You took those cues and formed the reaction.

Practically everything you come across becomes an idea in your head. The religion you follow primes you to act in a certain way. Your beliefs and the information you hold are also primes. The experiences and events in your life, your interactions with people, and even the actions you take also become memories that can be used in the future. For example, if you had an accident in the past involving loud noises, then you might grow up with the fear that your subconscious mind primed you with negative emotions or ideas even if you just heard a balloon pop nearby.

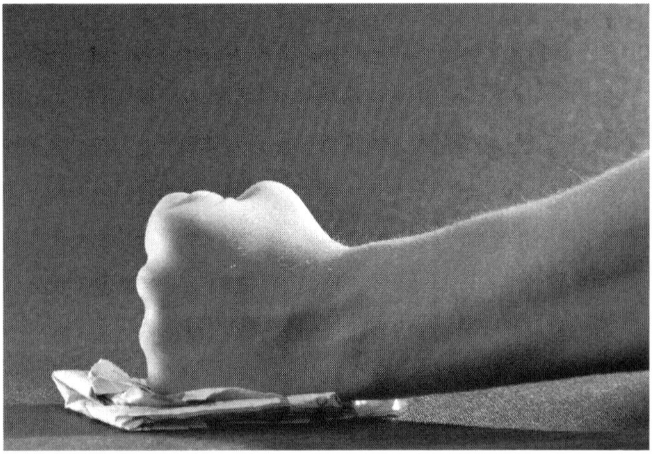

Image 6: Anger can sometimes be an involuntary action. You may not want to be angry, but you react instinctively.

The Power of Priming

When it comes to your fight-or-flight instincts, then priming becomes truly important.

Let's say that as you were growing up, you decided to adopt a pacifist lifestyle. You truly believed that non-violence was the way to truly live a wholesome lifestyle. One day in the future, you are confronted with a threat. Your fight-or-flight instincts kick in and you freeze. When your brain evaluates the situation, you realize that you are in the middle of a street brawl. You try to extricate yourself as stealthily as possible. Too late. One of the people involved in the brawl spots you. In response, you sit down on the ground and adopt a defensive position. You hope that you don't suffer too much damage.

The reason you reacted in such a manner during such a stressful situation is that your subconscious mind primed you with ideas of going on the defensive based on your past experiences, your personality, the ideas you have about violence, and many other factors. Priming is also one of the reasons why you freeze up, unable to do anything.

When you think about police officers who spring into action quickly when they sense danger, you often wonder how they do it. The reason for their quick reaction time is that they have trained their minds to forget over-analyzing things and jump into action. This response time is drilled into their physical and mental habits over and over again.

Now, the question is, how can you train yourself to react better? It's not like you are a danger magnet who always attracts catastrophes that allow you to keep trying the same scenario over and over again until you have mastered it. Certain situations might only occur once in your life while others might repeat themselves multiple times. But regardless of the situation, you want to make sure that you do not freeze on the spot or enter into a state of normalcy bias.

So, what do you do?

Let me ask you this question: Have you ever seen people who watch motivational videos or read thoughts in the morning? You might think those habits do not have any effect on the people. But in reality, they actually might.

When you enter your room and realize things are messy, then you suddenly experience a sense of exhaustion or disappointment. Some people actually become depressed after seeing their room in such a state. This influx of negative emotions eventually causes the person to become careless and lazy. Eventually, laziness has become part of their lives.

What do you think the solution to such a situation would be? You might say that perhaps it is best to start small. Try making your bed or organizing things properly every day. Make it a habit of doing these things. Eventually, you will become attuned to having a clean space that compels you to become a neat and tidy person. The constant drive to keep your room tidy and organized makes you an active person. Eventually, you form a nice habit. By making sure that you keep your room tidy, you have primed yourself to realize that cleanliness is a good thing. This, in turn, creates more positive primes and before you know it, you have created good habits for yourself.

When people watch motivational videos in the morning, they prime themselves to start their day on a positive note. Later during the day, if things did not go their way and they were going through a stressful scenario, their subconscious mind will automatically utilize the motivational video as a prime.

Positive primes create positive results.

Let us say that you are afraid of the dark. You know that if you were to see an odd shape, your first instinct would be to freeze instantly. Your solution would be to first analyze your fear. Then think of the ways that you can deal with it. For example, you could try going from room to room in the dark, testing yourself to be brave every night. You could ask your family member or friend for help. You could read books to help you teach yourself to overcome your fear. Eventually, the new ideas that you have formed about not being afraid of the dark become your prime.

Examine your life and think about the little habits that you would like to change. Do you procrastinate a lot? Then the next time you find yourself slipping into your thoughts, get up and do something. It could be anything small. But do it completely and finish the task. Move on to another task. This way, you will feel the satisfaction of completing your task. That satisfaction eventually becomes your new prime, overriding the previous prime that told you to not work and simply procrastinate.

Socially awkward? Try meeting new people. Feel like you would like to improve your physique? Head to the gym. As you change the things in the environment or perform little tasks, you eventually nudge negative primes away.

But how do these changes help you in a fight-or-flight scenario?

When you make enough positive primes, you gain a lot of positive traits in return. For example, going to the gym and working on your physical fitness boosts your confidence. This confidence becomes a positive prime. The next time you find yourself in a fight-or-flight situation, you are more confident about dealing with the threat.

When you start changing the way you live and the way you approach situations, you might just be able to create a positive prime that could be useful in the future.

Mobilization

And here, we return to the mobilization stage.

Based on your mental preparedness, you might either freeze completely, your thoughts running in different directions, or you might begin to analyze the situation in order to assess the threat.

Do note that even if you create positive primes, you might still freeze during the immobilization stage. This is a natural reaction that cannot be easily overridden. However, if you have trained your mind, then you won't remain in that stage for too long. You will not be rooted to a spot by fear or zoned out because of normalcy bias. You will become more decisive. Even if you choose to run, it is because you have analyzed the threat in the environment and have decided that it is better to flee than to fight.

The Characteristics of the Alert Zone

➢ Information Gathering

This is usually our first reaction; we freeze in order to absorb as much information as possible. Because we become alert, an area of the brain called the amygdala becomes hyperactive. Your amygdala is responsible for storing memories and emotions that you are able to use in the future for recollection and recognition. During the freeze stage, adrenaline is coursing through our body. This hormone stimulates the amygdala as well. The result is that your amygdala stores an extra set of memories. It takes in as many visual cues from the environment as possible to provide more information to the brain. This adding of memories is what causes time to slow down. You might have heard of people saying that when they were skydiving or trying some extreme sports, then the initial moments seemed to last longer. This is because their amygdala processed an extra set of memories, giving the illusion that time was slower.

➢ *Mobility*

Energy becomes diverted to those areas that require it the most. You feel mobility return to your limbs and you are able to move. When you decide to run, not only does your heart begin to pump blood to vital areas of your body, but your skeletal muscles relax, and your breathing quickens. The combination of all these reactions gives you more stamina than usual. You might have heard stories about people suddenly finding the stamina to run away from a wild animal or a parent who suddenly finds the strength to lift heavy objects in order to save their child. All of these situations explain the various physiological reactions that take place in your body to help you run or deal with a situation.

➢ *Digestion*

Our digestive process slows down. We do not need to absorb any more energy from food. The process of absorbing energy requires energy as well, energy that could be spent on other vital processes. The dorsal vagus is responsible for various digestive functions that take place below your diaphragm. When it realizes that we are facing a threat, it immediately stops those functions.

➢ *Puff-Up*

Evolution has taught has many things. Our ancestors would sometimes respond to threats by "puffing-up."

In this process, they would straighten their backs and necks, broaden their shoulders, and move their arms slightly away from their bodies. The reason for this is to appear bigger and more threatening than before. In a fight-or-flight situation, you might adopt this stance in order to create a threatening pose. It is a way to stop the situation from escalating by using fear and intimated to your advantage.

This "puffing-up" pose is usually utilized by people when conflict is unavoidable. They understand that there is no way to calmly resolve the situation and so they decide to prevent further damage to themselves by showing the opponent that they are not someone to be trifled with.

➢ *Guard*

Some people also take up a more guarded position. In this pose, they move their arms to protect their vital areas. Some even crouch or bend their knees in order to become a smaller target. They often clench their fists and tense their muscles. The muscle tensing is done in order to absorb impact better. A tighter muscle provides better resistance. Some people might even block their face.

All of these movements are a sign of preparation for conflict. In many cases, people might have extensive knowledge of self-defence skills. Yet they understand about weak points through numerous experiences in their lives. They fall back to what they know and do their best to make sure that are well-protected.

➢ *Belief*

Regardless of whether we choose to stand and fight or we choose to flee from the scene of the threat, each action is done so because, at some level, we believe that we are capable of surviving the incident. This is our brain's way of motivating us to do everything to make sure that we are safe. It wants the threat dealt with as soon as possible since your brain does not like prolonged periods of stress.

➢ *More Strength*

You are stronger than you realize. However, your body does not always use all of its strength. Your muscles use energy in an efficient manner. Why would it need to use all its strength simply to lift a coffee mug? It is inefficient and, at the same time, you become exhausted much more quickly. In many cases, your muscles also hold back on some of the strength in order to prevent damage. If you decide to punch a wall, your brain realizes that you might suffer terrible damage and even pain. In order to minimize the damage, it holds back on some of the energy you use.

However, in a fight-or-flight mode, your brain is not concerned about the energy. Its attention is focused on the threat. It knows that the threat could cause more damage and harm to you. If you choose to fight, then your brain releases the barriers that hold back your strength.

The Green Zone: The Social Engagement System

When the brain realizes that the threat has passed, then it relaxes. During the non-stressful situations in our lives, we are relatively healthy. Our bodies are ready for social engagement, we feel normal and at times happy, and we have entered the do-not-freak-out stage.

This stage is when the social engagement systems become active. However, I like to use a different term for it. I would like to call it the "connection stage." This is because it is during this stage that we either form new connections or develop the connections that we already have in our lives. We are able to walk around freely, have a nice conversation with friends, perhaps invite them over for dinner, spend time with family, and do various other sociable activities. As we have seen before, this stage of the fight-or-flight response is activated by the ventral vagus, which is also responsible for bringing us to a relaxed state.

A Sense of Safety

We feel safe when we realize that we can openly communicate with the people around us. It allows us to open ourselves to new ideas and emotions. But this sense of safety is more important than you might think.

Researchers at Google were interested in creating an environment where their employees work well with each other (Duhigg, 2016). They turned their attention to psychology in the hope that they would find their answers there. Fortunately, they did. But not in the way that you might imagine.

They didn't discover a fantastic psychological exercise or condition. Rather, they began to understand more about the social engagement system. As they researched further, they realized that the sense of psychological safety might just be more important than any other factor in order to create great teams. It helps remove unproductive actions and facilitates cooperation.

But how is the social engagement system able to achieve such results, especially within an organizational structure? What makes it so special?

The Power of Social Engagement System (SES)

Dr. Stephen Porges believes that when a situation pushes the state of mind to fall back on is primal behavior or fight-or-flight, that's when people suffer from trauma, misjudge social situations, or react in a manner that is not ideal for a particular situation.

Let us take an example of this. Imagine a person attending a social gathering. In the gathering, he is doing a good job of talking to people and keeping conversations going. Suddenly, he begins to feel a sense of panic. The fight-or-flight system has kicked in. Someone then approaches him with the aim of starting a conversation. Because the man is clearly not in a position to react in a sociable manner, he responds negatively. This negative response would not have happened if the feeling of fight-or-flight had never taken place.

In the research conducted by Google, it realized that in order to create better teams, it needed to prevent people from feeling threatened when they are within the organization. This means that they teach their employees to be more welcoming, have a friendly and open atmosphere, provide basic comforts, and even remove any form of discriminatory behavior. This prevents a person from being alarmed at every stage and reacting negatively towards others, thereby creating poor connections with others.

The SES is a sign that things are normal. When people fall back into a fight-or-flight stage, then they are constantly feeling tense. This causes them to increase the chances of falling into a traumatic situation. Psychologically, we are not always ready to deal with such a level of stress. Despite our preparations, every fight-or-flight situation leaves a psychological mark. When too many of these situations occur, then they might create a more permanent impact on our minds.

Think of it like taking a hammer and slowly tapping the walls. If you tap it a few times, then nothing might happen. But if you continue to tap it repeatedly, then at some point or another, you are going to leave a mark. Fight-or-flight situations are like hammer blows. Sure, you might be able to deal with some of them. But eventually, they are going to leave a mark on your psyche.

But what if you are really facing a threat?

We Return to Real and Imagined Threat

Remember what we talked about when we focused on real and imagined threats?

When you are truly facing a threat, then there are two ways to go about it. You deal with the threat or flee from it. When the situation forces you to face a threat, then you know your options.

However, there are times when the threat isn't real. It is merely a figment of your imagination or your thoughts on overdrive. During those times, it is easy for your mind to add stress for no apparent reason.

Over time, this could learn to long-term psychological conditions.

It becomes worse for people who already suffer from trauma or conditions like PTSD. When they fall into fight-or-flight situations repeatedly, the repeated stress prevents their recovery process and might even cause situations of relapse.

How Does the SES Help Us?

According to Dr. Porges, our SES allows us to pick up various signals from others. If the SES decides that what it has perceived is something that is non-threatening and even positive, such as a smile, a positive remark, or a pleasant interaction, then it immediately sends the signal to calm us down. Remember, the SES operates unconsciously. We are never aware of its influence. We have no idea that the SES can trigger or override the release of certain hormones that are caused by people or social interactions. This influence can be used in various situations, even in trauma therapy.

For example, think about groups such as Alcoholics Anonymous. The main theme of the group is about getting together and using a platform to find a way to control dependency on alcohol. In order to do this, the group does not rely on medications or surgeries. Rather, they use social reinforcements in order to help the people in the group cope with their condition. In such a situation, the SES becomes activated. It gauges the situation and realizes that it is in a safe environment. It recognizes the social cues from others, especially the support, encouragement, and other positive responses. It then takes these social cues to create a calming effect.

Other forms of psychological therapies, even when they utilize medications, involve social interactions. People with depression are asked to communicate with their family and friends. You will never see a therapist tell a sufferer of depression to take as much alone time as necessary. Rather, they encourage the individual to seek out positive relationships and find help from others. In many ways, the SES can be used for therapies.

This is how the SES can also be used to create a safe environment within an organization. When you realize that people might suffer from anxiety or stress because of certain social factors within the organization, then you can take steps to improve those situations in order for the person to feel safer. This improves overall morale and productivity.

The more researchers and psychologists understand about the SES, the more they realize that it is a powerful tool to create positive social environments, help people with psychological conditions, and even recommend people to live better lives.

The Characteristics of the Green Zone

➢ *Immune System*

Because the situation is normal, our immune system is not affected by stress. Your immune system consists of billions of cells that travel throughout your body. The main types of cells in the immune system are the white blood cells. There are essentially two types of white blood cells; phagocytes and lymphocytes. When there is no stress, these cells are able to move freely throughout the body and reach areas that require their assistance.

However, when stress increases, the body releases certain hormones called corticosteroids. These hormones play an important role in preventing inflammation and also provide assistance in the breakdown of fats. However, in order to prevent inflammation, they also suppress the immune system. When it suppresses the immune system, it also lowers the number of lymphocytes.

The lymphocytes in return are extremely crucial to our body's defense because they are responsible for recognizing antigens, destroying cells that could cause damage, and producing antibodies. By lowering the number of lymphocytes, the body lowers the level of antibodies and the chances of attacking a dangerous cell.

At the same time, stress also causes people to adopt unhealthy coping strategies such as drinking or smoking. This further affects the already affected immune system. Not only does the immune system have to deal with a lower supply of lymphocytes, but now it has to ensure that it fights any infections or problems that are caused by consuming or taking in harmful substances.

➤ *Joy and Curiosity*

We feel positive about the world around us. Our SES is in a non-relaxed state. So, it tries to seek out positive influences. This allows us to be happier and peaceful. We are more open to social encounters and we have a friendly aura about us. Now, when I say aura, I am not referring to anything that is metaphysical. When you look at a person and notice his or her aura, then the term is a reference to numerous factors; the person's body language, facial expressions, tone of voice, and reactions. When you look at these factors and judge them to be positive, then the person has a positive aura. Otherwise, the person has a negative aura.

In a relaxed state, you tend to have a positive aura. This positivity also makes you more curious about life. When we are stressed, we evaluate life negatively. We think that life is unfair and that it only causes suffering. Such thoughts lead to harmful primes. These primes, in turn, affect our outlook and motivation to do things. It affects our behavior, makes us feel hopeless, and even compels us to procrastinate a lot.

When there is no stress, we are able to look at the "bright side." We view life differently and try to be more thankful for our situation. We try to actively seek opportunities and are not afraid of making mistakes. Such behavior leads to positive primes, which are extremely useful to create positive changes to yourself.

➢ *Sleeping Habits*

Stress affects sleep patterns as well. You might find yourself lying bed feeling anxious and worrying about insipid affairs. You find out that you are unable to relax your mind, which makes it difficult to find the necessary level of quietness to fall asleep. This is also why people use the phrase "lose sleep over something."

When you are under a lot of stress, there are multiple thoughts vying for your attention. Each of them feels important. When you are unable to deal with any one of them, you feel a sense of disappointment, which makes you feel guilty, which further leads to shame, and well, the situation goes out of control. Soon, along with the stress, you have a cocktail of negative emotions swirling in your mind and you have no idea what to do or how to deal with them. All you can think of is simply closing your eyes and getting a good night's sleep.

Without all that stress to bog you down, you end up having a good night's sleep.

➢ *Eating Habits*

Fight-or-flight responses can affect our eating habits. During such intense stressful situations, we tend to ignore our hunger cues. Our brain is occupied with dealing with the source of stress. Prolonged ignorance of our hunger cues means that we don't eat for long stretches. There is a flip side to this situation as well and it is not a positive outcome. You see, there are people who end up consuming more food when they are facing stress. They use food as a distraction, consuming mindlessly without paying attention to what they are eating or how much they are eating.

But there is also another reason why you eat so much during a stressful situation. When you enter fight-or-flight response, your body releases the hormone cortisol, as we have seen earlier. This hormone also makes you crave salty, sugary, and fatty foods. The brain thinks that it might need energy in order to deal with the stress that it is facing. So far, it does not understand how stressful the situation is. Perhaps it could be nothing at all. But the brain continues to believe that it is about to spend a lot of energy to deal with the stressful situation. When that happens, people tend to pick up any snack or junk food that they can get their hands on. You might have seen people who are stressed eat an entire bag of salted chips without even knowing they did it. Or they could have glasses after glasses of soda, and they don't even realize that they are already on their third glass.

Image 7: What you eat affects your mood and emotions. A healthy diet can contribute towards a healthy mind.

➢ *Empathy*

A better SES allows us to read people well. We can understand them better and have the capacity to place ourselves in other people's shoes.

You might wonder why empathy is a difficult emotion to master. The reason is that there are a lot of thought processes involved when showing empathy. After all, we are trying to look at things from someone else's perspective. In order to do it properly, we need to think about their situation and then dig back into our memory to find a situation that is similar to the one faced by the other person. We then have to find commonalities between the two situations, allowing us to better empathize with the person. All of these steps require us to be in a better state of mind. If we are stressed, then we are more focused on dealing with the chaos in our own minds.

➢ *Attentiveness*

In order to be attentive, we have to be able to clearly perceive and understand what someone is saying. When our mind is free of stress, we do not have any distractions preventing us from listening intently.

Stress causes our mind to wander about our problems, challenges, and state of affairs. We are drawn to them like moths to flames. Our brain wants us to deal with them or perhaps find solutions to various problems. All of these form the distractions that keep us from truly connecting with someone else. And yes, your ability to listen well helps you form positive bonds with people. It shows that you are willing to use your patience to understand them or their point of view without prejudice or judgment.

- ***Calmness***

Most importantly, we feel calm. Our muscles are not feeling tense. The various parts of our bodies are relaxed. You are also able to communicate better since the ringed-muscles of your esophagus are more relaxed.

- ***Normal Digestive Process***

Your bowel movements and digestive processes begin to follow a normal routine. They function well. Your bowels are not emptying spontaneously. The food you eat is getting digested properly. You feel better and things have returned to normal.

A Social Metamorphosis

The SES is something that is unique to human beings. Scratch that. The SES is a system that has evolved considerably in human beings.

Animals do have a social system. They are able to understand and communicate with each other in a limited capacity. They can let each other know who the boss of a territory is, where to find food, hunt together, and perform many other social activities.

In humans, social expressions and forms of communications have evolved considerably. You only have to look at our communication capabilities to see how different we are from animals. But what exactly are these differences?

There are certain traits that give human beings the superiority in communication over other creatures on Earth. Now, I am not using the word "superiority" to show dominance. Rather, it expresses characteristics of human communication that denote more complexity, better expressiveness, and better emotional depth.

➢ *Creativity*

Human beings make use of linguistic resources to create new expressions, words, and sentences. They can arrange phrases, words, phonemes, and morphemes in such a manner as to communicate countless number of ideas.

Now, you might be wondering what phonemes and morphemes are. In any language, there are a fixed number of sounds. For example, the letter "o" is usually pronounced as "oh." The sound that you can produce with the letter is a phoneme. When humans combine the phonemes, they create a unit of sound. The smallest unit of sound that humans can create that contains meaning is called a morpheme.

For example, *car* and *dog* are the smallest units of sound because they cannot be broken down into anything. Other words, such as "understand" cannot be considered as a morpheme because you can break down the word into "under" and "stand."

➢ *Displacement*

Humans are capable of talking about imagined or real objects, places, and situations that are not present in their immediate vicinity. This means that you and your friends are capable of having a conversation about the incredible sights of Paris, what you should be doing next weekend, whether Marvel is better than DC, or if you should really purchase that Star Wars memorabilia that you have been thinking of. Animals, on the other hand, can only communicate about what they see in their immediate environment. For this reason, the communication methods of humans can be considered context-free, whereas animals don't have such freedom.

➢ *Cultural Transmission*

People are born into different cultures, can have different beliefs, and even learn different languages. However, that does not mean that they can be bound to those traits. They can transfer their languages and cultures onto others and they, in turn, can be influenced by other languages, cultures, and belief systems.

➢ *Interchangeability*

In human beings, communication can be interchanged between the sexes. Males and females can express in a myriad of ways and there are no gender restrictions on language. In certain animals, communication is restricted to a certain gender. For example, bees perform a dance to inform other bees about sources of nectar. This dance is restricted to the worker bees, which are female.

Alone, the SES system is a series of facial expressions. But together with our communication abilities and our capacity to show emotions, the system becomes a powerful tool to calm ourselves, engage in positive social interactions, deal with psychological issues and trauma, manage stress, and even form connections with others.

Because of the complexity of human communication, we are able to use the SES to explain so many social phenomena. For example, a study was conducted on the social skills of both male and female medical students before they entered medical school and again once they had completed their residency training (Taveira-Gomes, Mota-Cardoso, & Figueiredo-Braga, 2016). Almost all the students had gained a better ability to collect information or, in other words, they had become better researchers. However, the surprising part was that the students had lost their non-verbal communication capabilities. So, they were unable to form proper facial expressions or display positive body language and emotional patterns. The researchers could not figure out what was wrong. After all, the students were trained to deal with patients and had practice in real medical situations as well.

The Polyvagal Theory came to the rescue. The researchers found that the high-stress environment, where students have to sometimes work and study up to 18 hours a day, caused a deterioration of their social engagement system. In short, they were unable to use their SES and all the communication abilities they had to form positive social expressions and reactions.

This, in turn, resulted in the importance of teaching students better communication. However, medical institutions had no idea how to do it. In fact, in a study conducted in May 2019, researchers discovered that students themselves valued the importance of communication skills (Ruiz-Moral, Gracia de Leonardo, Caballero Martínez, & Monge Martín, 2019). But they had no idea how to introduce lessons and practices to improve such skills. The students mentioned that the addition of such lessons would only serve to make things more stressful to them.

From researchers to multi-billion-dollar organizations, SES has proven to be an important field of study for many entities. By combining SES with the complexities of human communication, psychologists and therapists can better help people cope with stress, trauma, and other psychological conditions.

And since we are on the topic of psychological conditions, it is about time we look deeper at those.

5:

STRESS AND THE POLYVAGAL THEORY

The Polyvagal Theory deals with much more than human expression. Since the vagus nerve is also responsible for managing the stress responses in the body and bringing it back to a normal state, psychologists and researchers have understood just how important the theory is for treating patients with psychological conditions.

What's more, the Polyvagal Theory can also be used to understand relationship issues and body languages. Let us look into these.

Understanding Trauma and PTSD

You can think of trauma as a wound. Yet it is a wound that one cannot see. It lies under the surface and is capable of causing pain and suffering to those who have to bear it.

Trauma is also a common threat to public health. According to the Substance Abuse and Mental

Health Services Administration (SAMHSA) branch of the U.S. Department of Health and Human Services, over 61 percent of men and over 51 percent of women have experienced at least one lifetime traumatic event. This event causes trauma that leads to lasting mental damages or debilitations that last the entirety of the individual's life. When taking into account behavioral health care settings, the statistics become even grimmer. Nearly 90 percent of clients in such settings have experienced trauma.

Trauma is not restricted to a particular demographic. It can affect people from all walks of life. But by understanding trauma, how it affects not just sufferers but their families, and the many ways people can seek support and assistance helps a lot in providing the right kind of help and treatment.

Causes of Trauma

Despite what people might think trauma is multifaceted. This means that the reasons for it are not always obvious and it could also be caused by numerous reasons rather than a single event. Most people are aware of those "shocking" events such as rape, accidents, loss of limbs, violence, robberies, and war. But not many people are aware that there are other situations that can cause trauma over time. These traumatic situations are often elusive because sufferers might actually act normal and for all intents and purposes, might continue to lead a relatively normal life. Situations such as growing up in a home where most or all members of the family are victims of addiction, show emotional abuse, constant instability in life, and poor mental health chips away at a persons' normal development.

Image 8: An accident can be a traumatic incident for many people. Some people might view the accident as a frightening experience and be able to get over it. Others don't have the mental fortitude to easily forget the situation.

In many cases, it might not be obvious that a person's present life choices are a result of past traumas. The results of trauma can sometimes be as complex to understand as the reasons that caused them. The important thing to note is that everyone is susceptible to experiencing trauma.

Traumas are formed when people are confronted by threats. We have already discovered what would happen when fear takes control of a person, causing them to freeze and be unable to deal with the threat.

We have also seen the results of an information overload, where normalcy bias cripples a person's senses.

But what happens when a threat takes over coping mechanisms and evokes feelings of pure terror, helplessness, and horror? In such situations, not only do individuals find themselves frozen on the spot, but they are unable to even rationalize what is happening to them. This situation might sound rather similar to normalcy bias, but there is a difference.

In normalcy bias, your brain is trying to normalize the situation. When you are faced with a traumatic experience, your brain is trying to explain the situation.

Your brain is facing a sight, sensation, or experience that is so detached from its normal viewpoint of the world. For example, soldiers who go to war experience violence on an unimaginable scale. Such violence sends their ideas on a tilt. Perhaps to those soldiers, a normal life would be Sunday barbeques, binge-watching Netflix, the Super bowl, late-night pizza with friends, and other similar activities that comprise a world that is far removed from violence and tragedy. All of a sudden, they are thrust into a situation where violence is amplified. It is as though someone cranked the violence dial to 100% and then found a way to go beyond it. The reality is jarring. It is shocking. And it has its effects.

These situations leave behind a mental scar.

Once these events occur, they become a permanent fixture in the minds of the sufferers.

People re-experience these traumatic events over and over again. The event might have occurred in the past, yet, whether frequently or occasionally, they overpower all other emotions, thoughts, and ideas in people. Sufferers often feel a lack of control and that can be scary and demoralizing.

And this brings us to Post-Traumatic Stress Disorder.

PTSD

When trauma continues to affect people for a long period, it constantly adds stress on the brain, especially when they are dealing with an extreme event. When this happens, there is a chance that people might suffer from Post-Traumatic Stress Disorder or PTSD.

Now, why did I use the word "chance"?

This is where things get a little more complex. Sometimes, it does not just depend on the frequency of the trauma, but the intensity as well. If someone were to experience trauma repeatedly, then there are chances that they might raise mental defenses to either block or reduce the effects of the trauma. These defenses prevent people from entering into a state of PTSD.

One of the best ways people can help themselves in the recovery process is through the use of SES. The core idea of SES is fairly simple. Less stress means better social interactions. More stress leads to poor social interactions. And it is these interactions that are beneficial in numerous ways, from having support groups to feeling less lonely. In many ways, having a positive social life benefits people in various, such as the ones listed below:

- Being social can reduce the chances of people developing depression. Not only is depression a debilitating mental condition, but it also makes traumas worse. People do not have a positive anchor to use. They enter a state of loneliness, isolation, and gloom. Sometimes, the situation escalates to such a degree that people contemplate suicide.
- Social interactions can reduce stress and even blood pressure. Now, you might wonder what the connection between social activities and blood pressure is. It has got more to do with stress. When you are in a state of stress, the body releases hormones that increase your blood pressure, as we had seen earlier. Imagine if your levels of stress did not decrease? Your blood pressure levels will also continue to remain high, leading to all kinds of health problems.

PTSD also leads to the following symptoms:

- People receiving stressful memories of the incident or incidents that had caused the trauma. These memories distract them from having a normal day.

- Nightmares affect people's sleep. In many cases, people resort to medication in order to put them to sleep properly. This, in turn, increases their dependency on prescription drugs.
- Certain moments create flashbacks of the traumatic event, making people feel as though they are reliving the entire event.
- People often feel like they are on edge. They are extremely jumpy and react to noises that are not threatening, such as a car passing by, the clink of glasses, or sometimes even the tap of footsteps.
- When reminded of the event, people tend to feel physically and emotionally bad. It is as though they are unsure who to blame, often turning the blame inwards and placing themselves in the crosshairs.
- People often have trouble concentrating on their tasks. They find themselves easily distracted. In fact, some people might have been able to put in all their concentration into their work prior to the traumatic event. After the event, however, the psychological and emotional stability is overthrown, and they take on new habits.
- There is a surge of negative feelings towards oneself. People place themselves in bad light. Some even consider harming themselves or worse, consider thoughts of ending their

lives. Substance abuse also becomes common among victims.

- All the activities that people used to consider normal don't seem to interest them anymore. They even avoid people to minimize the risk of trauma occurring again. They stay away from anything that even remotely reminds them of the trauma. For example, if a person experienced a traumatic incident in a movie theatre, he or she might refuse to enter a cinema in the future. In some cases, the person might even go so far as to avoid turning off the lights in his or her room when watching a movie at home.
- It becomes difficult for people to consider happy or positive thoughts, memories, and emotions. Even people who had a jovial character before the traumatic incident become moody, somber, and melancholy after the incident.
- People begin to display frequent outbursts of anger and rage.
- Memories become cloudy. Some people have trouble recollecting things that happened before or after the point of trauma. Few people block out the trauma entirely. Some people remember things differently, which happens when their minds are trying to minimize the damage of the incident on their psyche.

The Effect of Polyvagal Theory on Trauma and PTSD

The Polyvagal Theory has a two-pronged approach to dealing with trauma and PTSD.

➢ *Stress*

The first approach is to reduce instances of stress. People facing trauma have no idea when their bodies might go into a fight-or-flight situation. However, what they can do is to improve the body's resistance to stress. This is done by stimulating the vagus nerve. The sympathetic nervous system is responsible for triggering your stress response. To counter that, we have the parasympathetic nervous system. Stimulating the vagus nerve leads to the stimulation of the parasympathetic nervous system. This improves your stress resistance. Techniques like meditation, yoga, and even cold showers aid your vagus nerve and help you calm yourself even more.

The field of medicine has also developed technology to aid in the stimulation of the vagus nerve, but it is done in a rather unique way (McIntyre, 2018). Researchers are trying to see if they can combine technology and therapy. One of the ways that trauma patients are made to overcome their past is by making them relive the trauma and showing them that the traumatic incident has no control over their lives in the present. But what if the therapy could be taken one step further?

By using special technology, the vagus nerve can be stimulated while the sufferer's therapy is underway. As the patient relives the traumatic incident, the stimulation of the vagus nerve causes him or her to be calm. This, in turn, makes the mind of the patient believe that the traumatic incident does not have any effect on them. What could have taken multiple sessions with the therapist might now require fewer visits in order to get better.

➢ *Social*

The other facet of the treatment takes place on a social plane. This time, using the knowledge of SES, sufferers are asked to connect with people. They don't have to necessarily make new friends or jump into unknown situations. They can simply start socializing with people they already know. These people may include their family members, friends, or relatives.

You might remember that I had earlier mentioned that SES is all about decreasing stress in order to have a better social life. When you think about it, stimulating the vagus nerve has already led to less stress. This boosts the capacity to form positive thoughts, emotions, and expressions. All that is required after that is to start engaging in social situations. Being social allows people to participate in joyful and positive moments that help them overcome their trauma.

Understanding Dance of Attack and Withdrawal in Relationships

If you are or were in a relationship, then you might have felt this.

At some point in the relationship, there is a certain chill in the air. It feels as though you and your partner are walking on eggshells. Your approach towards each other is rather cautious. There is rigidity in your body language. You might attempt to say the right words, but you realize that the emotions that should convey the meaning of the words the right way don't exist anymore. It almost feels like you and your partner have become disconnected.

The thing you should remember is that the above situation happens in every relationship. People withdraw from each other, whether it is for a few minutes, hours, or even days. In some cases, the withdrawal can become a permanent position, which eventually leads to both parties calling it quits permanently.

By why do such withdrawals happen? And what exactly is the dance of attack?

Fear of Intimacy

It is not easy to be open to other people. You are revealing more about yourself and becoming vulnerable. The other person knows your strengths and weaknesses. As the relationship progresses, the more people get to know about each other. If people are not used to such levels of intimacy, then it is quite common for them to pause for a moment. This allows them to acclimate themselves to the shift in dynamics. However, if there is withdrawal due to intimacy very early in the relationship, then it could be a sign that the person is not ready to be in the relationship in the first place.

Rejection

This is a troubling situation people can find themselves in and it often leads to a never-ending loop. One person withdraws because he or she feels that it is far better to not put any risk into the relationship than make a move and then feel rejected. The other person sees the withdrawal as a rejection and decides that he or she should withdraw as well. Eventually, both parties have created a space that could have been avoided if they had communicated with each other.

Flooding

What might be rather tepid to one person might be pretty searing to another. What this means is that people are usually not on the same emotional level. To some people, emotions flood them in large quantities while others have stronger emotional resistances, where they have to deal with a trickle of emotions. When people become flooded with emotions, then it is not uncommon for them to withdraw back and take some time to deal with their emotions.

Image 9: When couples become withdrawn, they create a space between them that expands the more they choose to avoid each other.

Anger

You might have heard of the phrase "wear your heart on your sleeve." Well, some people also wear their anger on their sleeve. Others have trained themselves to hide their anger, preserving a more covert approach to dealing with their emotions.

Guess which of the above two forms of dealing with anger is more destructive? If you thought the fact that people openly display their anger is destructive, then you are right. If you concluded that those who hide their emotions are capable of more destruction, then you are right as well.

When people are quick to anger, they push their partners away, causing them to withdraw. Their partners feel like they have to constantly take careful steps in order to approach them. This causes their partners to remain in long periods of withdrawal.

On the other hand, people who allow themselves to steam internally become withdrawn. Rather than deal with the situation and communicate their feelings, they simply allow their anger to fester and take control of their rational thoughts. This does not mean that people should not take some time off to deal with their anger. Rather, they should ensure that they deal with their emotions and return to communicating with their partners or fixing any misunderstandings in the relationship.

Dance of Attack

In a dance of attack, both parties attack each other and then withdraw when they receive an attack in return. It happens when one person says something that is hurtful to his or her partner. The partner may or may not reply eventually, but they withdraw soon after.

After a while, the partner exits their state of withdrawal and then attacks the person. This becomes a loop where one person attacks, withdraws, steams in solitude, allows their negative feelings to fester, and returns to attack again. Each attack becomes more intense than the previous one because their negative emotions, thoughts, and ideas have escalated since their previous attack. Eventually, the situation becomes a case of "death by a thousand cuts." The meaning of the expression lies in the fact that during a sword battle, making small cuts on your enemy might not seem to cause a lot of damage in the beginning. Eventually, those small cuts begin to take their toll, wearing out the enemy until they meet their demise.

In relationships, making small attacks might not seem like a big deal at first. However, at one point, all those accumulated feelings and emotions might cause big damage. The individual might suddenly explode in a fit of rage, they might withdraw inward to such a degree that they might refuse to talk to their partners, or they might engage in activities that might betray their partner's trust.

Another form of the dance can occur in a different manner. One person withdraws while their partner makes a desperate attempt to make a grab. Those attempts might be intense at first, but the partner begins to wear out. The partner then decides to withdraw. Seeing this, the first person tries to exit out of his or her shell in order to make their own attempt at grabbing their partner before they withdraw completely. Eventually, this situation becomes a dance where each partner withdraws and attempts to grab.

Now, let us see how we can use the Polyvagal Theory to resolve the above situations.

Step 1: Take a Moment to Calm Down

Whether you are upset or hurt, try to calm your emotions. Vagus nerve stimulations allow people to find their center. Meditations are some of the most effective ways to soothe emotions that are roiling within you. Do not worry about the time it is taking to calm down. Some people are easily able to lower the intensity of their emotions within minutes while others might need a few hours.

Get more meditation tips and guide at http://liberty-books. online/get-free-meditation-guide/

Step 2: Prepare Yourself

Taking a cold shower, having a proper meal, and rinsing your mouth with cold water are all ways to stimulate your vagus nerve. A healthy meal plays an important role in our emotions as well. When we have high sugar and high cholesterol foods, then our moods begin to swing uncontrollably. Here's one way that could happen:

Some people experience a euphoric feeling when their blood sugar levels drop. This feeling creates slightly pleasant feelings. However, low blood sugar levels are not beneficial or healthy on a biological level. The body then tries to reverse this by releasing adrenaline, which is used to convert any glycogen into glucose so as to balance blood sugar levels. This release of adrenaline causes a fight-or-flight response, which in turn increases the stress levels in the body. Because of the sudden fluctuations in emotions, people tend to have bad feelings or irritability. And this is just one way that unhealthy food can affect your emotions.

Having a balanced diet helps your body to control its blood sugar levels, heart rate, blood pressure, and digestive processes. This, in turn, helps you manage your emotions and mental state.

Step 3: SES

We all know about the social engagement system by now. What is important to realize is that you can use it to your benefit to deal with problems in relationships.

Here are a couple of ways to use the SES.

➢ *Method 1*

You and your partner can try to engage in an activity that you both like. It could be watching an interesting movie, going out for dinner, or doing something that makes you both happy.

When you are engaged in such an activity, then you both can look at each other's positive emotions and help eliminate the negativity within you. Once you both feel better, you can sit down and have a proper conversation about the subject matter.

➢ *Method 2*

Spend some time with friends who can help you cheer up. You don't have to discuss the relationship problem with them. Rather, take the time to create positive emotions and feelings within you. Once that is done, you can then spend time with your partner to sort out the issue.

Three Step Process

In many cases, the couples might have to repeat steps multiple times in order to reach the desired outcome. Each time they use the steps, they help pivot their relationship in a new direction. A better direction.

Understanding How to Read Body Language

The Polyvagal Theory focuses on expressions since the vagus nerve is one of the many nerves responsible for controlling facial expressions. Your facial expressions are part of your body language. But they cannot be taken as the only representation of your body language.

For example, if someone frowns, you might think that they are perhaps showing disinterest or disapproval. What if they aren't? If you examine their other body language, then you might perhaps see that their arms are crossed. Then you should ask yourself what the two body language cues are trying to tell you. You might try and see if the room temperature is too cold for the person to bear. In which case, the person might be trying to keep himself or herself warm, and because they are unable to properly do so, they frown due to the slight discomfort they are feeling.

It is important to understand body language and there is a litany of works dedicated to the subject. However, we are going to go through some basic ideas about body language and what you should keep in mind while examining it.

The Eyes

The behavior and movement of the eyes can be very telling. When you are communicating with someone, try and observe the movement of their eyes and whether they are making direct eye contact with you or not. When a person is unable to make eye contact, then that could indicate disinterest, boredom, and sometimes even deceit. You can also check to see if the person's pupils have dilated or not. This could indicate if the person is responding to you in a favorable manner.

If a person is making a cognitive effort to interact with you, then the brain improves the senses, especially the auditory and visual senses. This is done in order to get as much information as possible from the listener. We cannot check to see if the person is interested based on their hearing abilities unless we hold the person's ears and peer into their ear canal, which I suppose won't be a socially acceptable action. The only remaining sign that you can use is the eyes and whether or not they are dilated.

Another factor that you can check is the person's rate of blinking. When people are stressed or they are thinking hard, they tend to blink more. In some cases, when a person blinks rapidly and touches the eyes or the mouth, then it could be an indication that they are lying.

Glancing can indicate a desire for that person or object. For example, if you are having a conversation with someone and they glance towards the door, then it could indicate that the person would like to leave. However, you cannot always assume something at face value. The person could have glanced at the door because something or someone outside piqued their curiosity. When it comes to people, glancing at them does not always indicate a sexual desire. Rather, when one individual looks at another person, there is a desire to talk to that person and nothing more.

Another thing to notice is that when people look up, it does not always mean that they are planning to concoct a story. They might be reaching deep into their memory reserves. At the same time, looking down does not always mean that the person is lying. They could be nervous or feeling socially awkward.

The Face

People can try and hide their facial expressions, but there are certain movements or reactions that are automatic. Try to pick out various non-verbal cues from the mouth to help you better understand the situation. For example, a simple smile can tell you so much about whether the person is genuinely interested or not.

As you might be aware, there are different kinds of smiles. A person can show a genuine smile or he or she can fake the smile. When people display genuine smiles, then they engage the entire face. It transforms them. You can often see it reflected in their eyes as well. Many people squint their eyes and some people even display folds (called crow's feet) at the corners of their eyes when they are smiling genuinely.

On the other hand, a fake smile is supposed to convey acceptance or pleasure without being supported by genuine feelings of acceptance or pleasure. You might have also seen an indication of the "half-smile" that only engages one side of the mouth. This indicates uncertainty or sarcasm.

The mouth can indicate other emotions and messages. A person might press their lips tightly. This is sometimes done when the person disapproves of something or shows displeasure, but he or she does not want to talk about it. Sometimes, lips that are slightly parted often show that the person is relaxed. You can confirm this by their body position and their overall mood.

The Head

Both the movement and the position of the head can send various signals. For example, the speed at which someone nods their heads in response to what you are saying could indicate their level of patience or lack thereof. If the person is nodding slowly, then he or she is interested in what you are saying. On the other hand, if the person nods repeatedly, then they want you to finish what you are saying as soon as possible.

Image 10: When you give an honest smile, it reaches your eyes and can transform your face.

Even head tilts can tell their own story. If the person tilts the head to the side, then that could indicate curiosity or interest. If the person tilts the head backwards, then they could be suspicious of you or might even disbelieve what you are saying.

Head movements can also indicate a person of interest or power. When you find yourself in a group, then you can easily say who is controlling the conversation, who is the most influential person in the group is, or who has the most power by looking at where most or all of the people are looking. Or, to be more precise, who they are looking at. You can also use this to find out people who are not considered important, disliked, or have much influence as well by seeing the person that most or all of the group members choose to ignore.

The Hands

People cannot control every part of their body consciously. If they choose to pay attention to their eye or head movements, then they might leave other actions to the subconscious mind. Those actions might become involuntary and automatic. The part of the body that people tend to "leak" non-verbal cues easily is the hands.

Hand movements can be used to read a person well, especially when combined with other non-verbal cues such as the eye and head movements. Look at the position of the hands when the person is sitting. Are they placing their hands on their laps, on their heads, or crossing them? These actions could indicate whether they are nervous, feeling cold, comfortable, or uncomfortable.

For example, if people place their hands over their heads, then it could be an indication that they are finding the conversation tedious or it could be that the position they are sitting in is rather uncomfortable. Using one hand to support the head while placing the elbow on the table indicates that the person is trying to get comfortable but is still interested in what you have to say. If the person uses both hands, then they are finding the conversation boring. However, in certain scenarios, placing the chin on both hands could indicate flirtatious behavior.

Final Tips

You can easily misunderstand a particular expression or non-verbal cue if you are unaware of the context in which it takes place. For example, if a person squints, then it could be that they are trying to analyze what you are saying in-depth. Perhaps they do not wholly trust what you are saying. But it could also be that you and the listener are sitting outdoors and there is a slight wind blowing dust and debris everywhere, some of which have entered the listener's eyes or are hitting his or her face.

During such instances, people have a natural tendency to protect their soft and vital parts. When you are examining the person's body language, make sure you are also aware of other factors that could affect them.

Some people might have a physical or psychological condition. Facial paralysis might make people seem like they are constantly frowning. When they attempt to smile, it might not look too genuine, even though the person is truly happy. Getting to know someone better helps you understand their reactions and body language clearly. Psychological conditions can also influence someone's body language. People who are facing depression or extreme stress cannot find it easy to show positive feelings and hence they should not be judged for that.

You can even influence people to show positive emotions. By being positive, you can help people lower their guard and be more open with you. Make sure that you combine different non-verbal cues to accurately conclude the emotional or mental state of the other person. Do not arrive at a conclusion because of just one non-verbal cue.

The Polyvagal Theory and Body Language

So, how is the polyvagal theory involved in all of this?

Most of the above areas that we covered, such as the eyes and the face, are influenced by the vagus nerve. When we understand the influence of the nerve, we are able to better empathize with people.

Why is the person unable to show a positive emotion? Could it be that he or she is either feeling stressed or had faced a stressful situation recently? Perhaps a livelier atmosphere could improve their mood. Maybe the conversation could focus on them so that they are able to express themselves more. Or you could ask them about it so that you and the other person can deal with the situation together.

Why is the person showing disinterest when they are usually interested in the topic that is currently being discussed? Could it be something as simple as hunger? When people are hungry, their blood pressure decreases. This lowers the energy levels in the body, including the energy required by the vagus nerve to control the expressions on the face. This is why you might notice that people look bored and uninterested before eating. But once they have satisfied their hunger, or even as they are chowing down on that delicious pizza and slowly gaining energy, they become more vigilant and enthusiastic.

Is the person currently feeling nervous or anxious? This could be an indication of their fight-or-flight mechanism in action. Their brains might have perceived an imaginary threat in the environment, and they are unsure of what that threat is. It could be something as simple as the temperature. People don't respond well when it is too warm. Maybe you could get them comfortable or relaxed. That way, they are able to reduce their anxiety and activate the vagus nerve to look at positive social cues.

As you can imagine, there are numerous reasons for a person showing negative emotions. Not all of them have to be for a nefarious reason. Understanding the Polyvagal Theory gives you a deeper insight into what compels a person to react in a particular manner. You come equipped with the tools to understand and read the situation and the person better.

6:

REDUCING ANXIETY, DEPRESSION, AND TRAUMA

The Polyvagal Theory is not just a cluster of information. It is a tool that can be used to improve one's physical, emotional, and mental well-being.

Let us examine the many ways that the theory can help us deal with anxiety, depression, and trauma.

Depression

Mental disorders like depression and anxiety are based, among many other factors, on the imbalances in the nervous system. I use the term "among many other factors" because it is never easy to pinpoint the cause of depression.

Depression can be hereditary. That might make some of the readers to pause and say, "Surely, you do not believe that author."

I understand the skepticism. If I were suddenly told that depression can actually pass from parent to child, I would wonder at the relationship between a mental condition and our DNA (which are essentially our building blocks).

However, a team of researchers have actually identified a gene responsible for carrying information about depression (Breen et al., 2011). The researchers further discovered that the gene could even lead to chronic depression, which is a severe form of the mental condition.

While depression cannot be easily diagnosed, it does not mean that we cannot do everything we can to treat it. Today, there are various therapies, medications, and lifestyle recommendations that help people cope with depression. One of the ideas for improving the conditions of depression sufferers is based on the Polyvagal Theory. In the case of depression, the functions of the sympathetic nervous system are prevalent while the vagus nerve is not allowed to put any influence. This means that the body is going through periods of calm to agitation and unrest quickly, which happens because the sympathetic nervous system becomes activated suddenly and the parasympathetic nervous system has to try and bring things back to normal.

In the case of depression, the vagus nerve is unable to cope with the sudden fluctuations caused by the sympathetic nervous system. Moreover, people with depression go through periods of extreme lows and highs. The reason it is happening is that the sympathetic and parasympathetic systems cannot properly estimate how much effort they should apply.

The sympathetic nervous system enters into a state of extreme stress and agitation, which causes the person to enter into a deep stage of depression. This is the extreme low that the person feels. At this point, the parasympathetic nervous system is doing everything to bring back the person to a normal mental stage. However, depression is not so easy to work with. Once someone enters into a stage of depression, they become plagued with negative ideas, thoughts, and memories. All of the negativity fuels the body's stress and anxiety levels, making them worse. This, in turn, affects the sympathetic nervous system to activate the fight-or-flight response, which worsens the stress levels, leading to more negative thoughts, and so on. The situation becomes a feedback loop and the parasympathetic nervous system has no way to create any positive changes.

Eventually, the parasympathetic nervous system gets the opportunity that it has been seeking. It cannot simply lower the levels of depression slowly, because there are chances that you could relapse. So, it does the one thing that it is programmed to do; it crash lands into a state of calm. This is where people feel a sense of high. There are so many good chemicals flooding their system that it almost feels euphoric. You might have heard stories about people who enter the high phase of depression spending erratically, engaging in harmful behavior, or making decisions without applying rational thought.

Eventually, all the good chemicals and positive feelings wear out. There is a moment when the positivity that existed suddenly begins to deteriorate, and that is the opportunity that the sympathetic nervous system is waiting for.

I am making the sympathetic nervous system seem like the villain in this book. But in reality, that is far from the truth. Your sympathetic nervous system is extremely important. Your fight-or-flight response is vital not just for your survival, but the way you function in your daily life.

Think about this situation: You are taking your driving test for the first time. You do not want to fail the test. The nervousness in your body has reached peak levels. As soon as you sit inside the vehicle, you notice that you have become increasingly aware of your surroundings. Your heightened sense of awareness allows you to spot details in the environment that you probably would not have in any other situation. This allows you to drive better.

From company presentations to challenging activities, your fight-or-flight instincts are there to give you the required boost that you need. Even rally drivers have a heightened sense of fight-or-flight, allowing them to make those hard turns carefully and make quick decisions to avoid colliding with a tree or causing their vehicle to roll down a hill. Think of your sympathetic nervous system as your superpower.

However, when it is not needed, it can become a problem. In cases of depression, when you have exhausted your positive feelings, your sympathetic nervous system takes over and then you fall back into a state of depression.

Breathing

One of the techniques that is being used to stimulate your vagus nerve is your breathing. When you are able to breathe deeply and calmly, you are able to supply more oxygen to your brain.

People forget to breathe properly. They often find themselves breathing shallowly, especially when they are nervous, stressed, or depressed. When you breathe properly, the brain becomes more active due to an influx of oxygen. This allows the brain to analyze the situation and reduces the fight-or-flight impulses that are currently active. That little help from the brain allows the vagus nerve to focus on bringing the levels of depression to a more manageable level.

Breathing also reduces the flow of cortisol, which is one of the main hormones that cause stress in the body.

Anxiety

People have heard this term uttered many times but are unable to explain what it really is. They know how to describe what happens when they feel anxiety, which is the increase in heart rate, the quickening of breath, and sometimes even perspiration.

But those are just the symptoms. So, how can one explain what anxiety is?

Anxiety is our body's response to stress. It is a state of mind where we are apprehensive, or we fear the things that are about to happen. Giving a speech in a large public space, going to school, or even finishing an important task can give people anxiety.

Now, you might think to yourself that the above situations don't exactly sound bad. In fact, they sound rather normal. And you are right. Anxiety is a normal part of life.

The situation becomes abnormal when your anxiety lasts longer than expected, such as a period of six months. In such cases, you no longer have anxiety. You have an anxiety disorder. And such a disorder can cripple your life.

The Constant Panic

Imagine that you are walking down a busy street and suddenly you feel a sense of fear. You look around you, but you only notice people on their way to perform their daily grind. You see no potential threat, yet the feeling of anxiety persists.

You reach your office, hoping to calm yourself down, but over the course of the day, your anxiety is barely manageable. After a week, you realize that something is wrong. You cannot even perform a simple task without feeling anxious about something. Even cleaning the dishes makes you anxious!

That is what happens to people who suffer from anxiety disorders. Some of the symptoms that they experience are:

- Frequent panic attacks, often when people least expect it. This makes people live in fear of the next panic attack.
- People might start to develop unnatural phobias, even though they never had those phobias before.
- They become extremely anxious in social situations. They believe that people are quietly judging them.
- Some people even develop anxiety when they are far away from the people they love or care about.

All of the above symptoms slowly affect the normal functioning of a person. They start making constant errors in judgment, are unable to maintain concentration, cannot keep their social life steady, and even find it unable to express themselves coherently.

Lowering Stress

When the body realizes that there is nothing for it to be worried about, then it stops being stressful. But how can one convince the body, especially the brain, that there is no threat in the environment? You might have guessed it; we simply lower the body's fight-or-flight instincts.

Panic attacks are mainly caused by your fight-or-flight response. So, to combat the situation, one begins to assist the other side to control the response and even reduce it considerably. And by the other side, I am referring to the parasympathetic nervous system.

Cold showers, gargling with cold water, exercises, deep breathing, yoga, and various other methods can be used to stimulate the vagus nerve. There are two benefits to this:

The first one is, of course, it lowers the levels of anxiety that we feel.

The second benefit is that we stop feeling anxious in situations where we used to be gripped by anxiety. Let's take an example. If you started receiving panic attacks in a subway station, then the station itself becomes a place of threat. Every time you are there, your panic attacks surface, making you feel anxious. However, by stimulating your vagus nerve, you learn to remain calm. When you enter the same subway station and you are actually in a calm disposition, then your brain recognizes that there is no threat in the station after all. This becomes a feedback loop and before you know it that becomes your default stance every time you are in the station.

When you remain calm in those situations that would otherwise cause you panic attacks, you are teaching your brain to evaluate the situation better. It is like talking to your brain and saying, "See? There is nothing here to be afraid of. It is just a station. I am calm. So, why should I start panicking?"

CONCLUSION

What once started as mere curiosity has been transformed into an entire field of study. Dr. Stephen Porges never knew that the area he would be focusing on would become an important discovery in the history of medicine and health. Even now, many of the features of the nervous system are still a mystery.

For example, the neurons form connections with each other by using certain mechanisms called axons. However, isn't it interesting that the axons know exactly where to go in order to make the right connections? How is that possible? How does one neuron decide which neuron it has to seek out? For a long time, the Polyvagal Theory was one of the mysteries of the nervous system as well. And it would have remained a mystery if it were not for a certain scientist who took particular interest in the vagus nerve.

The Polyvagal Theory is the next step in understanding our bodies and our health. Within just a few decades, we have understood so much about ourselves that we are able to effectively manage various physical and mental conditions. We are finding new and effective ways to treat old problems. And in the world of health and medicine, any new discoveries can lead to improvements in health and living.

If you want to see a paradigm shift when it comes to understanding human potential and dealing with trauma, emotions, and physical health, then the Polyvagal Theory is the next step in the evolution of medicine and science.

The theory is capable of properly understanding certain conditions, such as PTSD. When earlier, one of the common methods of dealing with trauma was to subject the sufferer to the traumatic incident and try to get them used to it; the Polyvagal Theory suggests that there is a better way to deal with things. It recommends using the traumatic situation in the healing process but also making sure that the sufferer finds himself or herself in a better state of mind.

The Polyvagal Theory allows us to properly listen to other people's experiences and understand them on a deeper level. Dr. Porges believes that the theory also allows us to connect with people better.

If we can think of the invention of the MRI, the recognition of yoga as beneficial to the health, and even the germ theory as landmarks in the development of medicinal and health practices, then it is not far-fetched to say that the Polyvagal Theory is the next landmark.

When you look at how much benefit it can provide in various fields, then it is safe to say that the more people look into it, the more they are able to discover new benefits and treatments to the human body.

Last but not least, if you haven't already, don't forget to grab your free meditation guide at http://liberty-books.online/get-free-meditation-guide/ and start activating your Vagus Nerve now.

REFERENCES

Bergland, C. (2014). Neuroscientists Discover the Roots of "Fear-Evoked Freezing." Retrieved 23 December 2019, from https://www.psychologytoday.com/us/blog/the-athletes-way/201405/neuroscientists-discover-the-roots-fear-evoked-freezing

Breen, G., Webb, B., Butler, A., van den Oord, E., Tozzi, F., & Craddock, N. et al. (2011). A Genome-Wide Significant Linkage for Severe Depression on Chromosome 3: The Depression Network Study. American Journal of Psychiatry, 168(8), 840-847. doi: 10.1176/appi.ajp.2011.10091342

Duhigg, C. (2016). What Google Learned From Its Quest to Build the Perfect Team. Retrieved 24 December 2019, from https://www.nytimes.com/2016/02/28/magazine/what-google-learned-from-its-quest-to-build-the-perfect-team.html?_r=0

Healthline. Aquagenic Urticaria: Causes, Symptoms, and Treatment. Retrieved 11 February 2020, from https://www.healthline.com/health/aquagenic-urticaria

Janssen, S., Arntz, A., & Bouts, S. (1998). Anxiety and pain: epinephrine-induced hyperalgesia and attentional influences. doi: 10.1016/s0304-3959(98)00060-8

McIntyre, C. (2018). Is there a role for vagus nerve stimulation in the treatment of posttraumatic stress disorder? Bioelectronics In Medicine, 1(2), 95-99. doi: 10.2217/bem-2018-0002

Panegyres, K., & Panegyres, P. (2016). The Ancient Greek discovery of the nervous system: Alcmaeon, Praxagoras and Herophilus. Journal of Clinical Neuroscience, 29, 21-24. doi: 10.1016/j.jocn.2015.10.047

Praderio, C. (2017). It's possible for one person to have two different sets of DNA — here's how it happens. Retrieved 11 February 2020, from https://www.insider.com/what-is-a-human-chimera-and-how-does-it-happen-2017-11

Roberts, C., & Bullis, C. (2019). Vagus Nerve Stimulation. Functional Neurosurgery And Neuromodulation, 109-112. doi: 10.1016/b978-0-323-48569-2.00015-x

Ruiz-Moral, R., Gracia de Leonardo, C., Caballero Martínez, F., & Monge Martín, D. (2019). Medical students' perceptions towards learning communication skills: a qualitative study following the 2-year training programme. International Journal of Medical Education, 10, 90-97. doi: 10.5116/ijme.5cbd.7e96

Taveira-Gomes, I., Mota-Cardoso, R., & Figueiredo-Braga, M. (2016). Communication skills in medical students – An exploratory study before and after clerkships. Porto Biomedical Journal, 1(5), 173-180. doi: 10.1016/j.pbj.2016.08.002